GANDHI
A Spiritual Journey

GANDHI
A Spiritual Journey

M.V. Kamath

Indus Source Books

Indian Spirit, Universal Wisdom

Indus Source Books
PO Box 6194
Malabar Hill PO
Mumbai 400 006
INDIA
Email: info@indussource.com
www.indussource.com

Gandhi: A Spiritual Journey

ISBN: 978-81-88569-11-3

Copyright © M.V. Kamath, 2007

First printed in 2007
First reprint 2015
Second reprint 2017

Front cover photograph: Dinodia Photo Library
Sketches of Gandhi by Aarti Padalkar

Material from works of M.K. Gandhi reproduced with permission of Navjivan Trust, Ahmedabad

Every effort has been made to trace the copyright holders and obtain permissions. Any omissions brought to our notice will be remedied in future editions.

All rights reserved

Printed at Jayant Printery, Girgaum, Mumbai 400002

This book is sold subject to the condition that it shall not by way of trade or otherwise, be lent, resold, hired out, or otherwise circulated without the publisher's prior written consent in any form of binding or cover other than that in which it is published and without a similar condition including this condition being imposed on the subsequent purchaser and without limiting the rights under copyright reserved above, no part of this publication may be reproduced, stored in a retrieval system, or transmitted in any form, or by any means, electronic, mechanical, photocopying, recording or otherwise, without the prior written permission of both the copyright owner and the above-mentioned publisher of this book.

In memory of B. G. Kher, a true Gandhian
with affection and respect

CONTENTS

	PREFACE	viii
1.	THE EARLY YEARS	1
2.	TRUTH IS GOD	41
3.	PATHS TO SPIRITUALITY	79
4.	UNITY OF ALL RELIGIONS	142
5.	A SPIRITUAL FORCE	184
6.	GANDHI AND GANDHIGIRI	193
	BIBLIOGRAPHY	198

PREFACE

I have written this book on Gandhi and his compulsive desire to attain spiritualism with a great deal of trepidation. It is seldom that one knows one's own self. How then can one presume to know the workings of another individual's mind—and that too, of someone like the Mahatma—with any degree of certainty? It is one thing to admit to one's fears and shortcomings and quite another to make an honest study of events and circumstances as are known and are public knowledge. Gandhi was by no means secretive about his thoughts and feelings and much to the discomfort and embarrassment of all his followers and even his close colleagues, had the courage openly to share them with one and all through his writings. The man was transparency personified. There was nothing that he hid from friends and foes including his wife Kasturba and his four sons. In the circumstances, it is difficult to categorise him. He is in a class by himself. There are literally scores of works on Gandhi, but the latest work entitled *Mohandas*, authored by his grandson Rajmohan Gandhi, tells us much more about the man than almost any other work of earlier vintage.

Gandhi's spirituality was not mere lip-service; it was rooted in positive action, for he was in every way a *karmayogi*. His spirituality consisted of identifying with the whole of God's creation and expressing it through tireless service of humanity. His journey towards realising the Supreme, therefore, encompassed a battle against untouchability, inequality, and all other prevailing unacceptable practices.

Spirituality underpinned all Gandhi's activities, whether social or political. He based his spiritualism on a strict moral code of conduct and ethics and it was due to his adherence to such a code that he could exercise a moral authority that not many can. What was remarkable about Gandhi, however, was his repeated assertion that every ideology had to submit to the acid test of reason before being accepted. He held that even the scriptures had to be rejected when they went against trained reason and the dictates of conscience. It was this questioning approach that led him to experiment with spiritual ideas, culminating in his definition: Truth is God. It is also this rational approach to religious beliefs and spirituality that makes Gandhi's ideals acceptable and practical.

However, for one who was so intensely conscious of spiritualism, a controversial part of Gandhi's spiritual journey has been his experiments with *brahmacharya*. Gandhi, let it be admitted, was obsessed with sex right from his teens and never seemed to have got over it even in his late seventies. That, by itself, is not unnatural as any psychiatrist will point out. Many sublimate their intense physical desires not by indulging in sex but by giving themselves to various forms of human activity that keep them busy day and night. Goodness knows Gandhi was busy enough. But for Gandhi, the sexual act was an obstruction in the quest for spirituality. He believed that it gave rise to passions and depleted a man of vital energy that could be put to better use. Sex, to Gandhi, also connoted a form of violence, which he was determined to weed out of his system. Spirituality, Gandhi held, consisted of awakening the higher and purer impulses in man.

What is surprising is that Gandhi, from what we know about him, had apparently never heard of tantric practices. In the work *The Essential Dalai Lama*, edited by Rajeev Mehrotra, a claim is made that "for Buddhism, sexual intercourse can be used in the spiritual path because it causes a strong focussing of consciousness if the practitioner has firm compassion and wisdom". Furthermore—and the quotation is from the book *How to Practice: The Way to a Meaningful Life* published by Random House—the point is made that the purpose of sexual intercourse "is to manifest and prolong the deeper levels of mind, in order to put their power to use in strengthening the realization of emptiness". The only explanation possible in the circumstances is that Gandhi was trying out one more of his acknowledged "experiments with Truth", howsoever defined. Can spiritualism be attained through a total separation of woman from man? Our gods have their consorts and even many of our saints and prophets were married or had women disciples. There is no reason why that should be considered a sin or an impediment to spiritualism. But Gandhi apparently had his qualms, which distract from his committed desire for spiritualism.

Many dismissed his *brahmacharya* as phony and nothing more than an effort to "cloak" his sensuality. Gandhi defended himself by saying, in an article in July 1938, that "any impure thought is a breach of brahmacharya [and] so is anger". He said he believed in the "sublimation" of "the vitality that is responsible for the creation of life" and that his *brahmacharya* "was not derived from books". Indeed, he added: "I evolved my own rules for my guidance and that of those, who, at my invitation, had joined me in the experiment." It doesn't sound convincing unlike the relationship he had developed with Saraladevi Chaudharani, a married woman with a son whom he wanted to have as his "spiritual wife", if such a thing ever existed. When, for all practical purposes, he left her, Saraladevi was shattered. As she later wrote: "[I] had put in one pan all the joys and pleasures of this world, and in the other Bapu and his laws and committed the folly of choosing the latter."

In the end one might well ask: What is spiritualism? The dictionary is of no help here. But if it means a way of reaching out to God, there are many ways of doing so without having to give up earthly pleasures. I leave it to every reader of this book to provide his own answer. Gandhi experimented with life and had his own explanations when confronted by his colleagues and friends. It is not for me to judge him. Gandhi is his own judge and jury. But because Gandhi is Gandhi, he cannot avoid being the subject of an inquiry into his essay into spiritualism. Gandhi provides a case study but I for one would not care to arrive at any conclusion; the jury is out and will for ever be out. He has seen to that by his own admissions. But of one thing I am painfully aware, that an accusation can be made that I have been selective in my quotations. That is the prerogative of an author. My only hope is that I have been fair to the Mahatma.

M. V. Kamath
Manipal, March 2007

1

THE EARLY YEARS

If there is one man who has had literally millions of words written about him, both when he was alive and even more importantly after he passed away, it is Gandhi. Mohandas Karamchand Gandhi. Gandhi, the Mahatma. Way back in 1966, in a talk given on the campus of the University of California at Berkeley, Prof. Eknath Easwaran made a remarkable statement. He was, of course, speaking about Gandhi. He said, "Historians of the future, I believe, will look upon this century not as the atomic age, but as the age of Gandhi."

Many of his listeners, including Michael N. Nagler who, in 1997, was to write a foreword to a book written by Prof. Easwaran on the Mahatma, were quite taken aback. Wrote Prof. Nagler: "I appreciated the sentiment, but it never occurred to me that the words were meant to be taken literally. Now I wonder. Every year, it seems, some prominent figure—the one most currently in the public eye is probably E. F. Schumacher—

steps forward to acknowledge the light Gandhi shed on his or her field."

To many people Gandhi was an enigma. Some, like the French philosopher Romain Rolland, had no doubt about Gandhi's essential role in life. Of the Mahatma he wrote:

> He has renewed, for all the peoples of the West, the message of their Christ, forgotten or betrayed. He has inscribed his name among the sages and saints of humanity; and the radiance of his figure has penetrated into all the regions of the earth.

Penderel Moon, who belonged to the Indian Civil Service and wrote an excellent study of the Mahatma entitled *Gandhi and Modern India*, was more down to earth in his assessment of the Mahatma. He wrote:

> Gandhi was both a politician and a saint, a combination of rôles not unusual in earlier epochs, but almost unique in the 20th century. He alone of front-rank political figures of our times claimed constantly and in public to be doing God's bidding, to be acting at the prompting of "the Inner Voice"; he alone sought to cast out devils and to win over opponents by prayer and fasting; and he alone made prayer-meetings a main avenue of approach to the public.

As to Penderel Moon, so to thousands, Gandhi was both a politician and a saint. However, Gandhi had no illusions about himself. Long after he was universally acclaimed a Mahatma he was to say, "I deny being a visionary. I do not accept the claim of saintliness. I am of the truth, earthy . . . I am prone to as many weaknesses as you are . . . I have gone through the most fiery ordeals that have fallen to the lot of man." And that came straight from his heart. Such was the awe in which Gandhi was held that on his death, Albert Einstein was to say, "Generations to come, it may be, will scarce believe that such a one as this, ever in flesh and blood, walked upon this earth."

Gandhi himself had no pretensions to Mahatmahood. As he wrote in *Young India*: "I do not feel like being one [a Mahatma]. But I do know that I am among the humblest of God's creatures. Often the title has deeply pained me . . . My Mahatmaship is worthless. It is due to my outward activities, due to my politics, which is the least part of me and is, therefore, evanescent. What is of abiding worth is my insistence on truth, non-violence and *brahmacharya*, which is the real part of me . . . Truth to me is infinitely dearer than the Mahatmaship which is purely a burden."

From his very childhood Gandhi showed his extraordinary allegiance to truth. He was born in a *bania* family and for three generations from the time of his grandfather they had been prime ministers in several Kathiawad States. Gandhi's father, Karamchand, alias Kaba, was also in his time the prime minister of Porbandar state. Kaba Gandhi married four times in succession, having lost his wife each time to death. His last wife, Putlibai, bore him a daughter and three sons, Mohandas being the youngest.

Mohandas claims that his father was truthful and brave but had very little religious training. However, Kaba made frequent visits to temples and listened to religious discourses. In his last days Kaba began reading the Gita and would repeat aloud some verses every day at the time of worship.

Putlibai, Mohandas' mother, was deeply religious. As he described her in his autobiography: "She would not think of taking her meals without her daily prayers. Going to the *Haveli*—the Vaishnava temple—was one of her daily duties. As far as my memory can go back, I do not remember her having ever missed the *Chaturmas*." *Chaturmas* literally means a period of four months, during the monsoon time, when many who observe it take a vow of fasting or semi-fasting. To quote Mohandas again: "She [his mother] would take the hardest vows and keep them without flinching. Illness was no excuse for relaxing them. I can recall her once falling ill when she was observing the *Chandrayana* vow, but the illness was not allowed to interrupt the observance. To keep two or three consecutive fasts was nothing to her." Even as a prime minister's wife, Putlibai was happy to live on one meal a day, during *Chaturmas*. It had become a way of life for her.

In a way, Mohandas was brought up in a house that was deeply religious. When he was still at school he chanced, one day, to come across a book bought by his father entitled *Shravana Pitribhakti Nataka* (a play about Shravana's devotion to his parents). At about the same time, he happened to see two itinerant showmen playacting the drama in which Shravana carries his blind parents on his shoulders on a pilgrimage. Both, the book and the action-play, left an indelible impression on Mohandas' mind. He said to himself, "Here is an example for you to copy." As he wrote in his autobiography about the play he had seen performed: "The agonized lament of the parents over Shravana's death is still fresh in my memory. The melting tune moved me deeply, and I played it on a concertina which my father had purchased for me." There was yet another play that was to make a great impact on Mohandas' life; it was *Harishchandra*, an embodiment of truth. He saw the play repeatedly and never tired of seeing it. He asked himself, "Why should not all be truthful like Harishchandra?" To follow truth and to go through all the ordeals Harishchandra went through was one ideal that inspired Mohandas. The story of Harishchandra touched him deeply. Although common sense told him that Harishchandra was more than likely a creature of fiction, he was almost convinced of the veracity of his existence. To Gandhi, both Harishchandra and Shravana appeared to be real characters and every fresh reading of their stories moved him to tears.

Interestingly, from his sixth or seventh year up to his sixteenth, when Mohandas was at school, he was taught many things except religion. Yet, he kept picking up things from his surroundings. Being born in the Vaishnava faith he often had to go to the *haveli*, but, significantly, it never appealed to him. He did not like its glitter and pomp. However, what he failed to get there was recompensed by his nurse, an old retainer of the family. Her name was Rambha. She was a dear, and like many old family retainers, was a source of comfort and security to the children of the family. Mohandas had a chronic fear of ghosts and spirits. Rambha gently convinced him that the best way to overcome that fear was to repeat *Ramanama* (Rama's name). In his autobiography, Mohandas says, "I had more faith in her than in her remedy, and so at a tender age, I began repeating *Ramanama* to cure my fear of ghosts and spirits. This was of course short-lived, but the good seed sown in childhood was not sown in vain. I think it is due to the seed sown by that good woman Rambha that today *Ramanama* is an infallible remedy for me." At about this time, a cousin of Mohandas who was a devotee of Rama, got him to learn *Rama Raksha*. Mohandas learnt it by heart and made it a rule to recite it every morning after a bath. He kept up this practice as long as he lived in Porbandar.

What left a deep impression on the mind of Mohandas was the way a great devotee of Rama read the Ramayana to his father at the time of his illness. The devotee was one Ladha Maharaj of Bileshwar who reportedly cured himself of leprosy by the regular reading of the Ramayana, repetition of *Ramanama*, and the performing of other rites. Besides, Ladha Maharaj had a melodious voice. He would sing the *dohas* (couplets) and *chopais* (quatrains) and explain them, losing himself in the discourse and carrying his listeners along with him. Mohandas was enraptured by these performances. That laid the foundation of his deep devotion to the Ramayana.

From Porbandar, the Gandhi family went to Rajkot, where the *Bhagavat* used to be read on every *Ekaadashi* (eleventh day of the bright and the dark half of a lunar month) day. Mohandas would sometimes attend the reading, although the reciter was often uninspiring. It was only much later, after hearing portions of the original read by Pandit Madan Mohan Malaviya, that he conceded that the *Bhagavat* could evoke religious fervour. In Rajkot, Mohandas got an early grounding in toleration for all branches of Hinduism and sister religions. His father and mother would visit the *haveli* as also temples devoted to Shiva and Ram. Jain monks would pay frequent visits to his father and he would listen to their discussions on subjects religious and mundane. His father also had Muslim and Parsi friends who would often drop by at their house and Mohandas would be privy to their talks. All these things together helped to nurture in Mohandas a feeling of toleration for all faiths.

Early in life Mohandas took a dislike to Christianity because, as he was later to write, he would often see Christian missionaries standing near the high school that he attended and holding forth, "pouring abuse on Hindus and their gods". Mohandas was also shocked to learn that a well-known Hindu got converted to Christianity and had to eat beef and drink liquor when he was baptised. The convert also went about changing his dress style from that of a Gujarati to that of a European, including wearing a hat. All this created in him an aversion to Christianity. At the same time, Mohandas had no living faith in god. He read *Manusmriti*, which was in his father's collection of books, but the story of creation did not impress him very much. On the contrary, it made him incline a little towards atheism. But one thing in the work took deep root in him: the conviction that morality is the basis of things and that truth is the substance of all morality. Truth, thereafter, became Mohandas' sole objective. This belief began to grow in magnitude every day and his definition of truth also began to widen.

At about that time, Mohandas came across a Gujarati didactic stanza that likewise gripped his mind and heart. Its precept—return good for evil—became his guiding principle. It became such a passion with him that he began experimenting with it in numerous ways. And let this be remembered, he was then still in his teens and attending school. The idea of conducting numerous experiments even at that age on the precepts laid down in that stanza certainly was a novel one. The origin of the title of his autobiography *Experiments with Truth* can probably be traced back to this period of his life. The stanza runs thus:

> For a bowl of water give a goodly meal;
> For a kindly greeting bow thou down with zeal;
> For a simple penny pay thou back with gold;
> If thy life be rescued, life do not withhold.
> Thus the words and actions of the wise regard;
> Every little service tenfold they reward;
> But the truly noble know all men as one,
> And return with gladness good for evil done.

Truthfulness had come to be part of Mohandas' life from a very young age. There is an incident which occurred during his first year at his high school in Rajkot that says a lot about him. An education inspector, one Mr. Giles, had come to inspect the school as part of his regular duties. He set five words for the students of Mohandas' class to write as a spelling exercise. One of the words was "kettle". Mohandas mis-spelt it. The teacher tried to prompt Mohandas to correct it by copying the spelling from a classmate sitting next to him. Mohandas declined to cheat. The result was that all the boys in the class, except Mohandas, were found to have spelt every word correctly. As he later reminisced: "Only I had been stupid. The teacher tried later to bring this stupidity home to me, but without effect. I never could learn the art of 'copying'. Yet the incident did not in the least diminish my respect for my teacher . . . For I had learnt to carry out the orders of elders, not to scan their actions."

The point is that Mohandas jealously guarded his character. The least little misdemeanour he might have indulged in would bring tears to his eyes. On one occasion, when he received corporal punishment, he did not mind the punishment as much as the fact that it was considered his just deserts. He wept piteously. On another occasion he was charged with lying—wrongly, as it turned out to be—and was fined. Writing about how hurt he was by this incident, he said, "That deeply pained me. How was I to prove my innocence? There was no way. I cried in deep anguish. I saw that a man of truth must also be a man of care." Subsequently, the fine was cancelled after Mohandas' father wrote to the teacher explaining why the charge of lying was wrong.

Mohandas' early years as he grew into manhood clearly show not so much his experiments with truth as the evolution of his spirituality. On this ground rightly can it be claimed in the words of Wordsworth that "Child is the father of man". Right from his childhood, Mohandas, perhaps even without his knowing it, was aspiring to a spiritual life. This striving for spirituality would lead him on a journey culminating in his own definition of God.

And it was not just Vaishnavism that affected his thinking. Jainism also exercised its influence on him to a substantial extent. In that sense, Mohandas was both born and brought up in the Vaishnava and Jain traditions. But those were times when the

British ruled India and British rule was considered inevitable because the Englishman was physically strong since he was a meat-eater. A doggerel composed in Gujarati by poet Narmad was very much in vogue then among students. It read:

> Behold the mighty Englishman,
> He rules the Indian small,
> Because being a meat-eater,
> He is five cubits tall.

But what had meat-eating to do with spiritualism? Nothing much except that it put Mohandas in a quandary, since meat-eating clashed with the pursuit of Vaishnavism, not to speak of Jainism, which totally abhorred non-vegetarianism. His parents, especially, were very devout Vaishnavites and would have been pained to learn that their son was eating meat. Worse, it had to be done on the sly. On the one hand was the conviction steadily growing within Mohandas that eating meat was beneficial, that it would make him strong and daring, and "if the whole country took to meat-eating, the English could be overcome". But to eat meat outside, he had to stop eating at home and that called for giving a false explanation, especially to his mother. It bothered him no end. He had to devise pretexts. As Mohandas was later to explain: "I knew I was lying, and lying to my mother. I also knew that if my mother and father came to know of my having become a meat-eater they would be deeply shocked. This knowledge was gnawing at my heart." In the end he was to abjure meat as food out of the purity of his desire not to lie to his parents. The desire to be honest and truthful won out in the end.

Then there was the time when a friend of his persuaded him to visit a brothel. Everything had been planned. The concerned prostitute had been paid in advance so that there would be no bickering towards the end. Mohandas recounted the incident in his memoirs: "I was almost struck blind and dumb in this den of vice. I sat near the woman on her bed, but I was tongue-tied. She naturally lost patience with me, and showed me the door, with abuses and insults. I then felt as though my manhood had been injured, and wished to sink into the ground for shame. But I have ever since given thanks to God for having saved me."

As with visiting the red light district, so in the matter of smoking, Mohandas' persona clashed with his pursuit of spiritualism. Then came one final fall from grace. Mohandas stole a bit of gold from his brother's armlet to pay off a debt. The debt, no doubt, was cleared, but the very act of stealing became more than he could bear. It began to haunt him night and day. Finally, he made up his mind to confess his action to his father. Mohandas recalls what happened in his memoirs and even just reading those few lines is enough to convey the poignancy of the struggle that went on in the young man's heart. The act of confession went as follows:

> But I did not dare to speak. Not that I was afraid of my father beating me. No, I do not recall his ever having beaten any of us. I was afraid of the pain that I should cause him. But I felt that the risk should be taken; that there could not be a cleansing without a clean confession.
>
> I decided at last to write out the confession, to submit it to my father, and ask his forgiveness. I wrote it on a slip of paper and handed it to him myself. In this note not only did I confess my guilt, but I asked adequate punishment for it, and closed with a request to him not to punish himself for my offence. I also pledged myself never to steal in future.
>
> I was trembling as I handed the confession to my father. He was then suffering from a fistula and was confined to bed. His bed was a plain wooden plank. I handed him the note and sat opposite the plank.

He read it through, and pearl-drops trickled down his cheeks, wetting the paper. For a moment he closed his eyes in thought and then tore up the note. He had sat up to read it. He again lay down. I also cried. I could see my father's agony. If I were a painter I could draw a picture of the whole scene today. It is still so vivid in my mind.

Those pearl-drops of love cleansed my heart, and washed my sin away. Only he who has experienced such love can know what it is.

At that point in time, Mohandas was sixteen.

———

Mohandas—henceforth he shall be called Gandhi—passed his matriculation examination in 1887. His elders wanted him to pursue his studies at college after the matriculation. He had two options: he could either go to Bombay, which was far away, or to Samaldas College in Bhavnagar, nearer home. Gandhi chose Bhavnagar, primarily because it was cheaper, but soon he found himself entirely at sea. College studies just did not suit him and at the end of his first term, he returned home.

The big question facing him was: What should he do? If college studies were out of the question and the thought of his doing medicine was unacceptable to his parents—fancy a good Vaishnavite dissecting dead bodies!—one option was still open: going to England to appear for the Bar examination. Indeed, that idea was even suggested by an old friend of the family, a shrewd and learned Brahmin who suggested to Gandhi's parents that they send their son to England. The friend argued that Gandhi would not have to stay in England longer than three years and that the expenses would not exceed four thousand rupees but the benefits would be enormous. Gandhi's mother was not very happy about the proposal. She had heard that

Indians in London took to meat and liquor—what if her son took to these vices? Gandhi had to tell her, "Will you not trust me? I shall not lie to you. I swear that I shall not touch any of those things." And he vowed that he would not touch wine, women, and meat. That settled the matter. The mother gave her permission.

Life in London was by no means easy. One problem was food. There was a Vegetarian Society in England with a weekly journal of its own. He joined it and shortly found himself on its executive committee. An elderly lady who befriended him introduced him to a bright young lady and matters soon came to such a pass that he had to confess that he was already married! Later, Gandhi was to say, "I thus purged myself of the canker of untruth, and I never thenceforward hesitated to talk of my married status wherever necessary." As for liquor, he never had much fascination for it anyway, so, in the end, he could stand by his vows and stay clear of wine, women, and meat.

Towards the end of his second year in England Gandhi came across two Theosophists who were interested in the Gita. They were then reading Sir Edwin Arnold's translation—*The Song Celestial*—and invited Gandhi to read the original with them. But Gandhi felt ashamed as till then he had read the Gita neither in the original Sanskrit nor in Gujarati and he had to admit to his ignorance. But he promised to do what he could and started with the Gita's second chapter. He was particularly impressed with *shlokas* 62 and 63:

Dhyaayato vishayaampumsah sangastshupajaayate
Sangaatsamjaayate kaamah kamaatkrodho bhijaayate
(Ch. II, *Shloka* 62)

Krodhaadbhavati sammohah sammohaatsmritivibhramah
Smritivibhramshaad buddhinaasho buddhinashaatpranashyati
(Ch. II, *Shloka* 63)

Gandhi read the translated verses as:

> If one ponders on objects of the sense,
> There springs attraction;
> From attraction grows desire,
> Desire flames to fierce passion,
> Passion breeds recklessness; then
> The memory—all betrayed—lets
> Noble purpose go, and saps the mind,
> Till purpose, mind, and men are all undone.

Gandhi was to say that it made a deep impression on him and the Gita itself struck him as one of "priceless worth".

With this reading it might be said that Gandhi's journey into the realm of adult spiritualism had begun. From that historic day onwards he was to regard the Gita as the book par excellence for the knowledge of truth, especially because it afforded him invaluable help in his moments of gloom. The two Theosophists thereafter recommended to Gandhi Sir Edwin Arnold's other book, *The Light of Asia*, which he read with even greater interest than he did the Gita. Once he started reading *The Light of Asia* he found to his surprise and delight that he could not leave it off. Delighted that they had found a pleasant companion, the Theosophist brothers led Gandhi to Blavatsky Lodge and introduced him to Madame Blavatsky and Mrs. Annie Besant who were to become household names in India in due course. Mrs. Besant had just then joined the Theosophical Society and Gandhi had been following the controversy about her conversion to Theosophy with considerable interest. The two brothers by then took courage to ask Gandhi to join the Theosophical Society but he declined the request as politely as he could, saying that with his "meagre knowledge" of his own religion he did not want to belong to any religious body. For all that, it was when he read Madame Blavatsky's *Key to Theosophy* that he felt stimulated to read books on Hinduism. Gandhi had begun to take the first steps on his long journey to understand truth and discover God.

For Gandhi, those days seemed to be ever so stirring. He chanced to meet a vegetarian Christian who persuaded him to read the Bible. He started with reading the book of Genesis and the chapters that followed, only to confess that invariably they sent him to sleep. But it was when he came to read the New Testament and especially Christ's Sermon on the Mount that he felt Christ's message going straight to his heart. Gandhi compared it with the Gita, when he read the verses which said:

> But I say unto you, that ye resist not evil;
> But whosoever shall smite thou on thy right cheek,
> Turn to him the other also.
> And if any man take away thy coat, let him have thy cloak too.

Gandhi felt reminded of Shamal Bhatt's famous lines: "For a bowl of water, give a goodly meal" etc. Wrote Gandhi of his experience: "My young mind tried to unify the teaching of the *Gita*, *The Light of Asia*, and the Sermon on the Mount. That renunciation was the highest form of religion appealed to me greatly." Reading the Sermon on the Mount whetted Gandhi's appetite for studying the lives of other religious teachers. A friend recommended to him that he read Carlyle's *Heroes and Hero-Worship*, which he did, but by then the time had come for Gandhi to appear for his Bar examination. Religious studies could wait. He had to fulfil the reason for coming to London first and foremost. That he did—and well, too.

When one speaks about spiritualism, what usually comes to one's mind is a person sitting in a yogic pose doing *dhyana* (meditation) or going to the temple to offer prayers or someone faithfully conducting rituals and observing fasts. Spiritualism, however, is much more than all this; it involves change in one's life, both internal and external, as Gandhi was to note of his years in London. As he walked further on the spiritual path he realised the necessity and importance of change, both within and without. There was one occasion, which he has faithfully recorded in his memoirs, when he almost succumbed to lust. He had to run away from the house where he had been accommodated as a guest, to save himself from obvious folly. It was during his stay in England that he realised that by itself religious knowledge was meaningless. It was also the time when he began to appreciate the significance of worship and prayer, concluding that they were much more representative of reality than anything else. He expanded this view in his memoirs:

> Such worship or prayer is no flight or eloquence; it is no lip-homage. It springs from the heart. If, therefore, we achieve that purity of the heart when it is "emptied of all but love", if we keep all the chords in proper tune, they "trembling pass in music out of sight". Prayer needs no speech. It is in itself independent of any sensuous effort. I have not the slightest doubt that prayer is an unfailing means of cleansing the heart of passions. But it must be combined with the utmost humility.

Gandhi strongly believed in prayer and had little respect for atheism. He recalls a time when he attended the funeral of a distinguished atheist Charles Bradlaugh, who was buried in Woking Cemetery. A few clergymen chanced to be present on the occasion to honour the dead. When they were waiting at a station to return home they were espied by a crowd of atheists, one of whom chose to heckle one of the clergymen.

"Well, sir," said he, addressing one of the priests, "do you believe in the existence of God?"

"I do," said the good man in a low tone.

"You also agree that the circumference of the earth is 28,000 miles, don't you?" came the next question.

"Indeed."

"Pray, tell me then the size of your God and where he may be?" the belligerent atheist continued.

"Well," replied the clergyman, "if we but knew, he resides in the hearts of us both."

"Now, now, don't take me to be a child," came the angry but triumphant response from the belligerent atheist but the clergyman this time assumed a humble silence.

Noted Gandhi, years later, recalling the incident: "This talk still further increased my prejudice against atheism."

Three years of legal studies went by quickly. Gandhi passed his examination and was called to the bar on June 10, 1891, at the young age of twenty-two. He enrolled in the High Court on the eleventh and left for India the very next day on the twelfth—reflective, no doubt, of his desire to return home as quickly as possible—feeling neither confident nor competent to practise law. The reason why his father's Brahmin friend had wanted Gandhi to be sent to England to study law was to make him eligible for the diwanship of Porbandar. If Gandhi's father, Kaba, could become prime minister with hardly any education to boast of, what could be beyond Gandhi's aspiration? But Gandhi had first to face some immediate hardships. Among Hindus of that period, going abroad or crossing the seas as it were, was a sin. When Gandhi returned home, the storm among the caste people over his foreign voyage was still brewing. It had divided the caste into two camps, one of which immediately re-admitted him into its fold while the other was bent on keeping him out. To please the former, Gandhi's elder brother took him to Nasik before going to Rajkot, got the England-returned to have a dip in the sacred river, and on returning to Rajkot, gave a caste dinner. Gandhi seems to have gone along with this *tamasha* with good grace out of love and respect for his brother although he did not particularly approve of it. However, it did put an end to the issue of his being re-admitted into the caste. But true to himself, Gandhi never sought to seek admission to the section of the caste that had refused it. Nor did he feel even mental resentment against any of the headmen of that section. He fully respected the caste regulations about excommunication. According to these regulations, none of his relations, including his wife's family could entertain him. And Gandhi himself would not so much as drink water in their homes. Gandhi was to say that they were prepared secretly to evade the prohibition but it went against his grain to do a thing in secret that he would not do in public. The result of this scrupulous conduct was that he never had occasion to be troubled by caste. Actually, he experienced nothing but generosity and affection from that segment of his caste that wanted him excommunicated. Gandhi may not have realised it at that time but surely this was his unconscious first experiment at non-violent non-resistance. As he was to write:

> It is my conviction that all these good things are due to my non-resistance. Had I agitated for being admitted to the caste, had I attempted to divide it into more camps, had I provoked the caste men, they would surely have retaliated and, instead of steering clear of the storm, I should, on arrival from England, have found myself in a whirlpool of agitation, and perhaps a party to dissimulation.

And then he started practising law. Or rather, he attempted to. He took up what was a "small cause" case. It had been referred to him by a tout and he was told that he had to pay commission to the tout, which, Gandhi, being Gandhi, refused to pay. He was told that even great criminal lawyers paid touts for bringing them clients, but Gandhi was adamant. He gave no commission but when he made his debut in Bombay's Small Causes Court he felt tongue-tied and could not argue. Finally, another lawyer was to do the pleading and win the case. It was an embarrassment that Gandhi took a long while to get over.

At his brother's suggestion, Gandhi closed down his office in Bombay and returned to Rajkot to practise law, earning an average monthly income of three hundred rupees. But even this did not last long. An offer came to do some legal work in South Africa that Gandhi found irresistible. He accepted it gladly.

Right from the start Gandhi realised that he would have to face problems. One of the first issues to confront him was the matter of having to take off his turban when facing a judge in court. Gandhi was willing to compromise but his Indian client felt that that would be succumbing to a white man's insult. So Gandhi took up the issue and was eventually allowed to stick to his turban. Then came an event of historical significance. It was also a leap frog in the development of Gandhi's spiritualism. It came about thus. On the seventh day after his arrival in Durban in South Africa, he left for Pretoria, duty bound. A first class seat had been booked for him. The train reached Maritzburg, the capital of Natal, at about 9:00 p.m. Bedding used to be provided at this station and a railway servant came up to Gandhi to inquire whether he wanted one. Gandhi declined, saying he had one. Then came a white passenger who started to stare Gandhi up and down. A minute later he went out to return accompanied by a couple of railway officials. Even before Gandhi could try to find out what the matter was came a third official who curtly told him, "Come along, you must go to the van compartment."

For a moment Gandhi looked non-plussed. He told the official, "But I have a first class ticket."

"That doesn't matter," came the reply. "I tell you, you must go to the van compartment."

At that point the conversation began to get a little heated. Speaking gently, as was his wont, Gandhi said, "I tell you, I was permitted to travel in this compartment at Durban. And I insist on going on in it."

The official wouldn't hear of it. He came straight to the point. "No, you won't. You must leave this compartment or else I shall have to call a police constable to push you out."

That was a threat and Gandhi was prepared for it. "Yes, you may. I refuse to get out voluntarily."

The inevitable happened. A constable was indeed summoned, who took Gandhi by the hand and pushed him out. His luggage was also thrown out. Gandhi refused to go to the van compartment as ordered and the train steamed away. Gandhi went to the waiting room and sat there, disconsolate. It was winter and severely cold. Gandhi's overcoat was in his luggage but he thought it wiser not to ask for it lest he was again insulted. He was, by then, shivering. There wasn't any light in the room and that only made matters worse.

Gandhi began to think. What was he to do? Should he fight for his rights or should he return to India? He had an obligation to fulfil—to argue his Indian client's case in Pretoria—and he was determined to do right by his client. So he swallowed the insult and took the next available train to his planned destination. From there he sent a telegram to the general manager of the railway who merely justified the conduct of the railway authorities. His client received him in Pretoria where he quickly learnt how Indians—all Indians—were treated roughly, and looked down upon as coolies. They were insulted frequently by the white man and had no recourse to social justice.

A year passed. Gandhi found himself drawn into fighting for the rights of the oppressed and the exploited. Already on a spiritual quest, this period of work strengthened the religious flame burning in him. Gandhi was to write:

> The year's stay in Pretoria was a most valuable experience in my life. Here it was that I had opportunities of learning public work and acquired some measure of my capacity for it. Here it was that the religious spirit within me became a living force.

Public work. It was more than that, it was public service. Indeed, it was even greater; it was finding the Lord in the service of the oppressed and the downtrodden.

There was once the case of a Tamil man in tattered clothes, head-gear in hand, two front teeth broken, and his mouth bleeding, standing in front of his office, trembling and weeping. He had been heavily belaboured by his white master under whom he was serving his term of indenture. What was Gandhi to do? First he sent the man to a doctor and obtained a certificate of the injuries suffered by the Tamilian. Then he took the Tamilian to a magistrate to whom Gandhi also submitted an affidavit. The magistrate was indignant when he read the affidavit and issued a summons to the Tamilian's white employer.

Word went around of Gandhi's noble move and he came to be regarded as a friend who could be approached by any indentured Indian labourer seeking justice. There is no doubt that at this point in time he was on his way to becoming a Mahatma—a saint.

Even if Gandhi then had no notion of sainthood, he was quite aware of his new assignment in life. He wrote later: "If I found myself entirely absorbed in the service of the community, the reason behind it was my desire for self-realization. I had made the religion of service my own, as I felt that God could be realised only through service. And service for me was the service of India, because it came to me without my seeking, because I had an aptitude for it. I had gone to South Africa for travel, for finding an escape from Kathiawad intrigues, and for gaining my own livelihood. But as I have said, I found myself in search of God and striving for self-realization."

At about this time, Gandhi came across Mr. A. W. Baker, who was attorney to his client, Sheth Abdul Ghani. Mr Baker was a staunch lay preacher and one of the directors of the South Africa General Mission. He had built a church at his own expense and he thought that with Gandhi's penchant for religious experience he could draw him into the fold of Christianity. So he gave Gandhi many religious books to read, besides the Bible. He also introduced Gandhi to some of his co-workers, one of whom was Mr. Coates, a Quaker. Coates was a frank-hearted man and practically loaded Gandhi with books on religion. Among them was a book by Pearson called *Many Infallible Proofs*. This was in support of the Bible as the author understood it. This book had no effect on Gandhi. Then there was another book by one Dr. Parker called *Commentary*, which, Gandhi conceded, was morally stimulating but was of no help to one who had no faith in the prevalent Christian beliefs. Then there was a book by one Butler entitled *Analogy*, which Gandhi found very profound but difficult to understand, obviously written to convert atheists into theists. The arguments advanced in it regarding the existence of God were irrelevant to Gandhi as he had, by then, passed the stage of unbelief. The arguments in proof of Jesus being the only incarnation of God, and the mediator between God and man, left Gandhi unmoved.

But Coates was not a man to easily accept defeat. He had great affection for Gandhi. He noticed Gandhi wearing a

Vaishnava necklace of *tulsi*-beads. Coates saw it as superstition and told Gandhi, "This superstition does not become you. Come, let me break the necklace."

That was some cheek. To that impertinence Gandhi quietly replied, "No, you will not. It is a sacred gift from my mother."

"But do you believe in it?" asked Coates.

"I do not know its mysterious significance," humbly replied Gandhi. "I do not think I should come to harm if I did not wear it. But I cannot, without sufficient reason, give up a necklace that my mother had put round my neck out of love and in the conviction that it would be conducive to my welfare. When, with the passage of time, it wears away and breaks of its own accord, I shall have no desire to get a new one, but this necklace cannot be broken."

But the missionary in Coates could not accept Gandhi's thinking. How could he? After all, Coates wanted to deliver Gandhi from what he thought was the abyss of ignorance. Wearing of *tulsi*-beads to keep harm away or to acquire merit seemed an irrational practice. As Coates saw it, salvation was impossible for Gandhi unless he accepted Christianity. To Coates that was *the* truth. He told Gandhi that his sins, such as they were, would not be washed away except by the intercession of Jesus and that all good works were useless. There was pressure on Gandhi from some of Coates' friends, known as the Plymouth Brethren. Their arguments on the nature of sin and the surety Jesus gave in providing redemption to the sinner were totally unacceptable to Gandhi. Tired of being talked down to, Gandhi finally had to tell the Brethren that their concept of Christianity was such that he could not accept it. Firmly, he told them, "I do not seek redemption from the consequences of my sin. I seek to be redeemed from sin itself, or rather from the very thought of sin. Until I have attained that end, I shall be content to be restless."

For all the pressure brought on him by the Brethren, Gandhi was not much disturbed and it did not prejudice him against Christianity. What Gandhi found unappealing about Christianity was the way in which the Bible was interpreted. He also saw nothing novel in the stories of the Christian saints or any profound philosophy in Christian theology. As a Hindu, he had already been exposed to the concept of sacrifice, which, to his mind, was much deeper than the Christian understanding of it. He therefore found it very difficult to accept that the only path to attaining Godhead was through Christianity.

In his book *A Gandhian Theology of Liberation*, the Jesuit priest, Rev. Ignatius Jesudasan S.J. notes that the openness of Gandhi's mind and the earnestness of his search are clear from the religious correspondence he carried on, not only with Hindu authorities in India but with Christian authors in England, as well as from the discussion of his dilemma with Kalicharan Banerji, a prominent Christian congressman at Calcutta in 1901. At that time, Gandhi, who was thirty-two years old, was seeking to convince himself of the objective truth of Christianity. But, as Rev. Jesudasan saw it, even Kalicharan Banerji failed to convince Gandhi that the only way of deliverance was surrender unto Jesus. Gandhi also met prominent Brahmos, read Brahmo literature, and even met Vivekananda's devotee, Sister Nivedita, with her "overflowing love for Hinduism".

It would seem that the works of two authors helped to crystallise Gandhi's beliefs. One of them was Edward Maitland, author of *New Interpretation of the Bible* and co-author of *The Perfect Way*, a repudiation of the then current Christian belief. Both the books helped support Gandhi's own faith in Hinduism. The other author was Leo Tolstoy whose books *Gospel in Brief*, *What to do*, and *The Kingdom of God Is Within You* overwhelmed Gandhi and "left an abiding impression" on him. *What to do* inspired Gandhi with its profoundly reflective thought and open truth and it quite clearly overshadowed all the books given to him by Mr. Coates.

Of Gandhi and his concept of Christianity Rev. Jesudasan writes:

> Gandhi's image of Christ was an inclusive one, which both confirmed and challenged Gandhi's Hindu paradigms, and therefore which, in Christianizing him on Gandhi's own terms, did so not by alienating him from his Hinduism but by making him a better Hindu. Though Christ was not for Gandhi the only begotten Son of God, he was a singular source of inspiration. In this sense, Gandhi's own life is a more likely witness to the uniqueness of Christ than that of many a conventional Christian.
>
> Gandhi, like no one else before him, showed on the stage of world history that the process of liberation can be so Christian in style and inspiration as to demand the values symbolized by the cross. His example and his teaching might well be a factor in all political action and in all political and liberation theologies.

Gandhi could accept Jesus as a martyr, an embodiment of sacrifice, and a divine teacher but not as the most perfect man ever born. As Gandhi saw Christ, his death on the cross was a great example to the world, but Gandhi did not think that there was anything like a mysterious or miraculous virtue in it. Philosophically, too, Gandhi saw nothing extraordinary in Christian principles.

It was not Christian missionaries alone who sought to convert Gandhi. Even his Muslim friends made attempts to convert him to Islam. Gandhi obtained books on the subject and even purchased a translation of the Koran and read it. He was in regular touch with a friend, Raychandbhai, in Gujarat, who would send him books to read. They included *Panchikaran, Maniratnamala, Mumukshu Prakaran* of Yoga Vashishtha, and

Haribhadra Suri's *Shaddarshana Samuchchaya*. Of all the efforts he put in his search for truth, he was grateful to all who tried to show him the way. Of them he was to write:

> Though I took a path my Christian friends had not intended for me, I have remained for ever indebted to them for the religious quest that they awakened in me. I shall always cherish the memory of their contact. The years that followed had more, not less, of such sweet and sacred contacts in store for me.

For all that, Gandhi was quite clear about his views on religion. Tendulkar, in his biography of Gandhi, quotes him as saying:

> There was a time when I was wavering between Hinduism and Christianity. When I recovered my balance of mind, I felt that to me salvation was possible only through the Hindu religion and my faith in Hinduism grew deeper and more enlightened.

He was aware of the many shortcomings of Hinduism, like the practice of untouchability. Gandhi never believed that untouchability was an element of Hinduism and went further to categorically disown Hinduism that advocated untouchability. He was also totally opposed to conversion. He said in his writings:

> Supposing a Christian came to me and said he was captivated by reading of *Bhagavat* and so wanted to declare himself a Hindu, I should say to him: "No, what the *Bhagavat* offers, the Bible also offers. You have not made the attempt to find out. Make the attempt and be a good Christian."

That, in a profound sense, indicated the levels of spirituality that Gandhi had attained. As we shall see later, to him religion meant adhering to values, not a brand name. God was to him truth; indeed, he was later to say that truth is God. Gandhi believed in service to the poor and the *dalits*. Service to man was, to him, equivalent to service to God. But over and above everything else was Gandhi's belief and adherence to truth.

Gandhi's quest for truth—and for God—continued till the end of his days. Importantly, he recorded his journey in his writings. Before he started his weekly, *Harijan*, he was editing *Young India* in which he confided his innermost thoughts. As was stated before, Gandhi was opposed to conversion. He was appalled when the British press put out a story that a British Admiral's daughter, Miss Slade, who had joined Gandhi's Ashram and was re-named Mirabai, had embraced Hinduism. Writing in *Young India* (February 20, 1930) the Mahatma wrote:

> I may say that she has not. I hope she is a better Christian than when four years ago she came to the Ashram. She is not a girl of tender age. She is past thirty and has travelled all alone . . . I have had the privilege of having under me Musalman, Parsi and Christian minors. Never was Hinduism put before them for their acceptance. They were encouraged and induced to respect and read their own scriptures . . .
>
> We have in the Ashram today several faiths represented. No proselytizing is practised or permitted. We recognize that all these faiths are true and divinely inspired . . . Miss Slade bears not a Hindu name but an Indian name. And this was done at her instance and for convenience.

Gandhi was frequently being asked about religion, the religion that he professed, and the reason why he wanted to remain a Hindu. He called himself a *sanatani* Hindu. He used the word *sanatana* in its natural sense. *Sanatana* means eternal or everlasting. *Sanatana* Hinduism is belief in the Vedas, the Upanishads, the Puranas, and all that forms part of Hindu scriptures, and therefore in avatars and rebirth. It also means belief in the *varnashramadharma* in a strictly vedic sense, as an evolving concept and not in its present popular and crude sense. In fact, by 1936, Gandhi declared that there was no varna, that caste had to go, and that all Hindus were equal. *Sanatana* Hinduism also encompasses cow-protection in its larger sense of preservation of the entire sub-human world and realisation of man's identity with all that lives.

Being a *sanatani* Hindu did not require Gandhi to accept as authentic everything that passed as Shastras. He rejected everything that contradicted the fundamental principles of morality. He said that he was not required to accept the *ipse dixit* or the interpretations of pundits. As Gandhi saw it, in a concrete manner he was a Hindu who believed in God, immortality of the soul, transmigration, and the law of karma and moksha. He tried to practice truth and ahimsa in daily life and therefore practised cow-protection in its widest sense, and understood and tried to act according to the law of *varnashramadharma*. Confident of the nurturing tolerance of Hinduism, he said:

> It is the good fortune or the misfortune of Hinduism that it has no official creed. In order to protect myself against any misunderstanding, I have said that truth and non-violence is my creed. If I were asked to define the Hindu creed, I should simply say "search after truth through non-violent means". A man may not believe even in God and still call himself a Hindu. Hinduism is a relentless pursuit after truth and if today it has become moribund, inactive, irresponsive to growth, it is because we are fatigued and as soon as the fatigue is over Hinduism will burst forth upon the world with brilliance perhaps unknown before. Of course, therefore, Hinduism is the most tolerant of all religions. Its creed is all-embracing.

It was not just a "relentless pursuit after truth" that made Gandhi what he was. It was also a relentless pursuit of fairness and justice that gave meaning and content to his life. Early in 1894, following the successful conclusion of the legal case to fight which he had been invited to South Africa, Gandhi was preparing to return to India when his client, Sheth Abdullah, insisted on giving him a farewell party. In the course of this party Gandhi noticed a newspaper article headed "Indian Franchise" which revealed that a bill was about to be introduced in the local legislature disenfranchising all Indians in Natal. Gandhi's instincts for fairness and justice were immediately aroused. He suggested to Sheth Abdullah and others present that the outrageous bill should be strenuously resisted. If that was not done, he said, Indians in Natal would lose even such few rights as they then enjoyed. But the Indians felt that they had no leader to fight their case. Would Gandhi mind staying for a while longer so he could give fellow Indians a sense of direction? As Gandhi was later to say, "The farewell party was thus turned into a working committee . . . Thus God laid the foundations of my life in South Africa and sowed the seed of the fight for national self-respect."

The fight for asserting self-respect among Indians was on. Volunteers were enrolled. A petition was drafted. Signatures were collected. Quite a stir thereby was created. Newspapers began to take notice of this development. Though the bill was passed, it became clearer by the day that Indian immigrants would not take it lying down. What Penderel Moon was to describe as "a monster petition" was thereupon drawn up for submission to Lord Ripon, a former viceroy of India, who was then secretary of state for the Colonies. Ten thousand signatures were obtained in a fortnight. As it eventually turned out, the Disenfranchising Bill was disallowed. For Gandhi it was a triumph but by then pressure started building up on him to continue to stay in Natal. There was the question of making a decent living. Gandhi wanted to serve the people and did not want a paid job. In the circumstances, some twenty leading Indian merchants decided to keep Gandhi on a retainer to do their legal work. The Law Society of Natal was opposed to his being admitted as an advocate of the Natal Supreme Court but it was over-ruled. Gandhi had to make but one concession and that was to remove his turban when appearing in court.

Professionally, Gandhi was satisfied with what he was earning. But he was still ill at ease. He longed to do some humanitarian work of "a permanent nature". So the young barrister found time to serve in a small hospital. That meant ascertaining a patient's complaint, laying the facts before the doctor, and dispensing the prescriptions. It was hardly what Gandhi was trained for. But he was quick to realise that his hospital service brought him in touch with suffering Indians, most of them indentured Tamil, Telugu, or North Indian men. Commenting on this aspect of his life, Gandhi later wrote: "Thus service of the Indians in South Africa ever revealed to me new implications of truth at every stage. Truth is like a vast tree, which yields more and more fruit, the more you nurture it. The deeper the search in the mine of truth the richer the discovery of the gems buried there, in the shape of openings for an ever greater variety of service."

It was "variety of service" that he sought. When the black plague broke out in the squalid Indian ghetto of Johannesburg, the sick and dying were taken to an abandoned, quarantined building where a heroic English nurse spent long hours alone, caring for them. One evening, at the height of the epidemic, she saw a small figure standing at the door. "Get out, this is plague!" shouted the nurse. But the man standing there was Gandhi whom the nurse recognised as a leader of the Indian community. He was not about to leave. He told the nurse, "It's alright; I've come to help you." And he went straight to the sick. One man was literally covered with vermin and the nurse again shouted a warning. She told Gandhi, "Leave him." But Gandhi would not. He merely told the nurse, "He is my brother." And he stayed all night long until relief came.

There was another such instance, which Gandhi recorded: "The question of further simplifying my life and of doing some concrete act of service to my fellow men had been constantly agitating me, when a leper came to my door. I had not the heart to dismiss him with a meal. So I offered him shelter, dressed his wounds, and began to look after him."

The ideal of selfless service had taken hold of Gandhi and was to cause rapid changes in every aspect of his life. Soon, he gave up a European style of living. It was not an easy thing to do. But the spirit of selfless service was beckoning and the call was irresistible. As he pushed forward with zest towards his new goal, his joy knew no bounds. Everywhere he began to see two paths open to him; to live for himself alone or to live for others. He chose the second option. He made time for voluntary nursing even in the midst of a busy legal practice. To propagate his views he started a weekly news journal called *Indian Opinion* and when the Boer war broke out he recruited an Indian ambulance corps. It attracted a lot of attention and a handful of dedicated young men and women, both European and Indian, came to live with him and share in his experiments in the art of living.

Gandhi's writings in *Indian Opinion* too started attracting attention and one of those who were drawn towards the journal was Henry Polak, a Jewish journalist. Polak introduced Gandhi to John Ruskin's *Unto This Last*, a book that cast a magic spell on Gandhi and brought about "an instantaneous and practical transformation" in his life. He was later to translate the book into Gujarati with the title *Sarvodaya* (The Welfare of All). It not only confirmed Gandhi's philosophical convictions but it also gave Gandhi some practical ideas. Inspired by its exaltation of manual labour, Gandhi bought a hundred-acre orchard at Phoenix, near Durban, to start a new life of service.

From *Sarvodaya* to satyagraha was a major step and it happened this way. It was the policy of the British Administration to limit as strictly as possible, the entry of new Indian immigrants into the Transvaal. With that in view, a draft Asiatic Law Amendment Ordinance was published in the Transvaal Government Gazette whose provisions were to shock Gandhi as much as all resident Indians. The ordinance required all Indian men, women, and children over eight years of age to register with the authorities, submit to finger printing, and to accept a certificate which they were to carry with them at all times. Penal provisions were prescribed for non-compliance with any of these provisions. The ordinance, which came to be known as the Black Ordinance, had to be fought and it was decided that a deputation led by Gandhi should go to London to argue the Indian case before the secretary of state for the Colonies, since Transvaal then was still a British Colony. The British Government sounded sympathetic but within a few months of Gandhi's visit the Transvaal was granted responsible government and it ceased to be a Crown Colony. Having attained a new status, the Government of Transvaal quickly passed the Black Ordinance which thereafter became an Act totally to the detriment of the interests of Indians. Indians now had no other option but to fight it tooth and nail.

How was the fight to be conducted? Gandhi did not believe in violence. Violence, in any form, was abhorrent to him and under no circumstances would he have advocated it. To him, non-violent resistance was the only way out. But how was this to be achieved? The approach had to be worked out in great detail. The first thing that had come to Gandhi's mind was to call his movement one of "passive resistance". But the phrase did not express the real essence of the movement. It was a negative expression and it also indicated inaction. Gandhi disliked what was an essentially Indian movement to be dismissed in so vague a term. There was nothing "Indian" about it. What was worse, Gandhi discovered that the term "passive resistance" gave rise to what seemed to him to be a "terrible misunderstanding". At a public meeting in Johannesburg, one Mr. Hoskens, a European sympathiser had spoken of passive resistance as "a weapon of the weak" to which Indians, having failed to secure redress by other means, were compelled to have recourse because they were few in number and without arms or votes. It was true enough that Indians were few in number. It was equally true that they had been deprived of votes. But Gandhi wanted to convey, both to his European friends and equally to his European foes, that the Indians were by no means weak and had, what he considered, "spiritual force" which was stronger any day than muscle power or arms. He therefore did what seemed the most natural thing to do. He advertised in *Indian Opinion*, seeking a proper title for the movement that he was to launch. Suggestions understandably poured in, especially since a prize had been offered for the most acceptable title. Maganlal Gandhi coined the word *sadagraha*. As suggestions go it wasn't a bad one; it meant firmness in a good cause. But Gandhi's mind, always tuned to truth, caught on to a new and parallel term: satyagraha. *Sat* means truth and *agraha* implies firmness, a combination of which would serve as a synonym for force—non-violent force. It was a stroke of genius. Explaining this to his friends, Gandhi said, "I then began to call the Indian movement 'satyagraha', that is to say, the force which is born of Truth and love or non-violence."

Gandhi took great pains to clarify that satyagraha differed from passive resistance in that it abjured all kinds of physical violence, not just as a matter of expediency but as a matter of principle. As Penderel Moon so beautifully described it:

> In ordinary passive resistance physical force is eschewed because it appears to offer no hope of success; but it might be used if suitable occasion arose for it. In Satyagraha physical force is altogether forbidden even in the most favourable circumstances. Gandhi maintained that Satyagraha also differed from passive resistance because in the latter there is always present the idea of harassing the other party, whereas "in Satyagraha there is not the remotest idea of injuring the opponent. Satyagraha postulates the conquest of the adversary by suffering in one's own person".

The Buddha may have demanded eschewal of violence. So did Mahavira, but Gandhi took the principle to new and greater heights of excellence.

Now came the first implementation of satyagraha and it was to turn into a historic occasion. The Government opened registration offices under the Black Act for Indians to register their names. The date: July 1, 1907. Gandhi had sent word that no Indian should present himself at these offices and volunteers were asked to stand close to the offices to dissuade any Indian who might be inclined to apply for an immigration permit. The volunteers were told that they must behave politely and respectfully to the police if they tried to interfere with the picketing. That was an essential part of satyagraha. Volunteers worked enthusiastically but not always successfully, considering that some Indians privately intimidated those of their kind who were inclined to take out permits. For a time the satyagraha seemed to work. According to one calculation, as many as nine thousand Indians refused to apply for permits as laid down by the Black Act. At that point, the Transvaal government decided to make arrests. To start with, just one Indian, and a man of no particular stature, was arrested and sentenced to one month's simple imprisonment. It had no effect on the Indian community. Somewhat frustrated, General Smuts, the minister who was handling the imposition of the Black Act ordered the arrest of a number of prominent Indians who were told that if they failed to comply with the provisions of the Act they would have to face retribution. None complied. Along with Gandhi they were produced before the Court and Gandhi himself was sentenced to two months' simple imprisonment. True to his nature, Gandhi requested the magistrate to award him at least the three months' imprisonment imposed on others, along with hard labour and a fine. That was Gandhi all over, a spiritual leader in the fullest sense of the term. Others then offered satyagraha and some 150 Indians were sentenced to imprisonment. And many more were getting ready to follow suit, when Gen. Smuts began to realise that satyagraha actually worked and could not be taken lightly. So Gen. Smuts agreed to come to terms with Gandhi and the Indian community.

A charming story of the encounter between Gandhi and Gen. Jan Smuts is recalled in this connection. Gandhi told the Boer leader gently but firmly, "I've come to tell you that I am going to fight against your government."

Somewhat taken aback, Smuts said, "You mean to say you have come here to tell me that?" And before Gandhi could answer, he added, laughing, "Is there anything more you want to say?"

"Yes," said Gandhi, smilingly, "I am going to win!"

Smuts was astonished. Dumb-struck! "Well," he said at last, "and how are you going to do that?"

Back came the instant answer, "With your help!"

Years later, Smuts was to admit, and not without humour, that that was exactly what Gandhi did.

As satyagraha promised to reach higher and higher heights, Smuts agreed to a compromise. While he insisted that the Europeans in the Transvaal wanted the law (the Black Act) to remain on the statute books, he would agree to the compromise as suggested by many other Indian leaders. According to Gandhi, Smuts said:

> I have consulted General Botha also. I assure you that I will repeal the Asiatic Act as soon as most of you have undergone voluntary registration. When the bill legalizing such registration is drafted, I will send you a copy for your criticism. I do not wish there to be any further recurrence of trouble, and I wish to respect the feelings of your people.

Gandhi considered it fair, but as time passed, Smuts reneged on his promise. And a fresh satyagraha seemed called for. Following Smuts' promise the satyagraha had been withdrawn but Gandhi soon found that the Europeans who were in power in the Transvaal were bent on stopping all fresh Indian immigration as if the Transvaal was land given only to the Whites. Gandhi wanted equality with the Europeans and thus began the second phase of satyagraha.

This consisted of all Indians who had received their registration certificates publicly setting those certificates on fire and ready to face any outcome. So, in a large cauldron set up in the grounds of the Hamidia Mosque in Johannesburg, more than two thousand registration certificates were thrown into the fire. The Transvaal government reacted by arresting some Indians and deporting them. Gandhi once again faced arrest and a second term of imprisonment, and when he had undergone that and was released, his fellow Indians decided that he, along with a Muslim colleague, Sheth Haji Habib, should go to London to plead their cause. Nothing much came out of it, except some practical concessions which had nothing to do with racial discrimination.

Gandhi returned to South Africa in November 1909 by ship and during the long voyage, wrote a pamphlet *Hind Swaraj* (Indian Home Rule) in his own words "in order to demonstrate the sublimity of satyagraha". The pamphlet was not specifically addressed to the problems of Indians in South Africa. Rather it was the first time that Gandhi formulated some of his basic ideas on how to face up to injustice and alien rule. His writing focussed on his seminal thought that stayed with him till the end of his political life. Fundamentally, the pamphlet criticised European civilisation for its materialistic leaning, expressing appreciation for Indian civilisation, which, Gandhi believed, was underpinned by spirituality and faith in God.

Even when he was handling political problems, Gandhi was not forgetful of spiritual growth. In the course of the satyagraha that he had initiated, he had received the support of scores of Indian immigrants whose lives of intermittent imprisonment had precluded them from earning a regular livelihood.

How was he to keep the families of those imprisoned from starving? A timely donation of twenty-five thousand rupees from Sir Jamsetji Tata, who had come to know of Gandhi's great effort to restore the rights and self-respect of Indian immigrants in South Africa, helped. Gandhi was then living in the Transvaal. His own ashram in Natal, the Phoenix Ashram, was three hundred miles away and was of no use to help families living in the Transvaal. It was at this point that a well-to-do German admirer of Gandhi, Kallenbach, an architect by profession, came forward with meaningful help. He put at Gandhi's disposal, free of rent, a farm of about 1100 acres, abundantly stocked with fruit trees, about twenty-one miles from

Johannesburg. This was the best support Gandhi could possibly have got.

At about that time, Gandhi was in touch with Tolstoy, whom he held in high regard, and as if to commemorate this event, Gandhi named his new Ashram after Tolstoy. It was in Tolstoy Farm that Gandhi continued with his satyagraha experiment with remarkable success.

Soon after establishing Tolstoy Farm, Gandhi invited his small band of faithful satyagrahis to build simple houses for themselves under Mr. Kallenbach's direction. This was self-help in the best sense of the term. The satyagrahis engaged in working on the farm, and in such activities as carpentry and sandal-making. Gandhi himself later learned to make sandals and made a special pair to be presented to Smuts. In the evenings, all the inmates got together for prayers and sang hymns in English, Hindi, and Gujarati. At its peak period, Tolstoy Farm had as many as sixty-six inmates and at the lowest there were barely sixteen. But that didn't bother Gandhi. Numbers did not matter to him. Service did. As far as Gandhi was concerned, Tolstoy Farm was to be a centre of spiritual purification and penance for the final campaign.

He was visited by none less than Gopala Krishna Gokhale, the eminent leader from India, whom Gandhi accepted as his political guru. Gokhale's visit culminated in a two-hour meeting with the Transvaal leaders, Generals Botha and Smuts. It was then that yet another compromise was arrived at, with the Transvaal Government agreeing to repeal the Black Act. Gandhi was sceptical. True, the government did repeal the Black Act but not the three pounds tax which had been levied on Indians.

Meanwhile, another issue had arisen to raise the shackles of Indians. In March 1919, the Supreme Court of the Cape Province delivered a judgement, which seemed to invalidate in South Africa, all marriages not celebrated according to Christian rites. This "bastardising" of all Indian children whose parents had been married according to Hindu, Muslim, or Zoroastrian rites was highly offensive and the Indian community reacted angrily. Once again, Gandhi decided to initiate satyagraha. This time he could get the cooperation of over five thousand men, women, and children, who, acting on the advice of Gandhi, decided to proceed to the Transvaal by way of protest. The Government reacted swiftly and arrested Gandhi, released him, and re-arrested him, sentencing him to nine months' imprisonment. But the power of satyagraha was too much even for Gen. Smuts. He could have handled a violent demonstration very easily and been proud of his success but what could he possibly do with a non-violent and highly disciplined gathering of men, women, and children who would not even lift a stone to throw at the police? So the government of the Transvaal appointed a commission of three members, which, after much discussion, produced a report recommending that the main Indian demands, namely, repeal of the three pounds tax and validation of Indian marriages, should be accepted. Gandhi's satyagraha—call it non-violent non-cooperation—succeeded. The Transvaal Government gave effect to the Commission's recommendations in the Indian Relief Act. Thus, after nearly eight years of continuing, but often interrupted, satyagraha, Gandhi had won self-respect for his poor countrymen in racist South Africa.

It was not violence but his spiritual approach that had won the battle. In that sense, it could be said that Gandhi's work in South Africa had ended. It was now time for him to return to India. He had lived in South Africa for twenty-one long years. Those were years of turmoil. But those were also years of spiritual preparation which were to stand him in good stead in the years ahead. Gokhale had asked him to return to India where more work awaited him. Gandhi accepted Gokhale's advice and took himself and his family to London on his way back home—to India, where he belonged.

"The saint has left our shores," Gen. Smuts said smugly, and added, "I sincerely hope, forever."

That hope, as far as Gandhi was concerned, was fulfilled. He was never again to return to South Africa.

2

TRUTH IS GOD

Before we proceed to elaborate on what Gandhi did after his return to his homeland it may be pertinent to discuss some of his views on the meaning of truth and his concept of God. For, in the end, what mattered most to Gandhi was not politics but the relentless pursuit of truth.

Time and again he tried to define truth. He conceded that God could not be described in his fullness and that any description of him would fall short of reality. As he once said:

> To me God is Truth and love; God is ethics and morality; God is fearlessness. God is the source of Light and Life and yet He is above and beyond all those. God is conscience . . . He is a personal God to those who need His personal presence. He is embodied to those who need His touch. He is the purest essence. He simply is to those who have faith. He is all things to all men. He is in us and yet above and beyond us."

Gandhi did not perceive God as a person. For him, God was a living, timeless representation of life itself. He rued the fact that though God pervaded everything and everyone, only some had the capacity to find succour in his abundant grace. On another occasion he said:

> Truth is the first thing to be sought for, and Beauty and Goodness will then be added unto you.
>
> As regards God, it is difficult to define Him; but the definition of truth is deposited in every human heart. Truth is that which you believe to be true at this moment and that is your God. If a man worships this relative truth, he is sure to attain the absolute Truth, i.e. God, in course of time.

Gandhi accepted that the road to God-realisation was not easy. He described the path he was following as one "straight and narrow" and said that it was like walking on the edge of a sword. He must have remembered the saying in the Kathopanishad:

> *Kshurasya dhaaraa nishitaa duratyaya*
> *Durgam pathasthat kavayo vadanti*
> (Ch. III, *Shloka* 14)

(The wise say that following the path [to atman] is as difficult as walking on the razor's edge.)

And yet he seldom faltered. Even when custom or tradition permitted him to utter untruth when he was practicing law, he never wavered. Gandhi would have been forgiven if he had been less than completely honest in the interests of his clients as others in his profession were wont to be. But he chose the path of truth. Very often, appearing in matters of public interest, he charged nothing beyond actual expenses. Gandhi's goal was never to acquire wealth or rise to the top in his practice at any cost. He was absolutely clear that his conscience mattered more than anything else. It was this clarity that helped him stand firm and adhere to his principles.

God is Truth, Gandhi used to say till 1931 when he began to say, Truth is God. As he put it, "Denial of God we have known. Denial of truth we have not known. The most ignorant among mankind have some truth in them. We are all sparks of Truth. The sum total of these sparks is indescribable, as-yet-unknown Truth, which is God."

Gandhi insisted that even an atheist believed in truth and concluded that God is the atheism of the atheist. This explanation he further explored thus:

> Truth is God—nothing else, nothing less. The nearest word answering to Truth in Sanskrit is *sat*. *Sat* means being. God alone is *sat*. He alone is, nothing and no one else is. Everything else is an illusion. *Satya* means *sat*. Truth alone is in the world, nothing else is. This is easy enough to understand. Then what is truth? For us it is a relative term. Absolute Truth is God. Whatever we understand by God is implied in Truth."

When asked to define the characteristics of truth, Gandhi had very definite thoughts. Truth, to his way of thinking, was the only lasting reality, which brought permanent happiness. Truth was pure, eternal bliss. It was knowledge; it was the force one felt within. In short, without truth, there was nothing.

Gandhi's argument was that those who believe in God's guidance do the best they can and never worry. Had the sun ever been known to suffer from overstrain? And yet, Gandhi asked, who slaves with such unexampled regularity as he? Gandhi's adherence to truth was immeasurable. Gandhi believed that truth and God are one and the same. He admitted to being overwhelmed by the many forms and definitions of God but he reiterated that he worshiped him only as truth. Although he admitted that he had not yet found God, he was ready to give up everything in his search for him, even his life. But his conviction that truth personified God was strong and he would continue to hold to it until he had realised the Absolute Truth. But even when he admitted that he had not yet found God, he recalled that often in his progress he had "faint glimpses of the Absolute Truth, God" and daily the conviction grew upon him that God alone was real and all else unreal. Gandhi was ready to share with everyone the basis for his conviction. He hoped that others would find merit in it and be convinced for he believed that the means of searching for truth were simple enough for anyone to follow. The only essential ingredient was humility; for what was easy enough for even a child could be insurmountable for an individual full of false pride. It was Gandhi's view that if we had attained the full vision of truth, we would no longer be mere seekers, but have become one with God, for truth is God. But, he went on to say, being only seekers, we prosecute our quest and are conscious of our imperfection. Pursuing this thought to its logical conclusion, Gandhi pronounced that our own imperfection made us incapable of comprehending religion in its perfect form and prevented us from finding the Absolute.

Gandhi argued that religion of our conception, being thus imperfect, was always subject to a process of evolution. And if all faiths outlined by men were imperfect, the question of comparative merit did not arise.

Gandhi had no doubt that truth was revealed in all religions but that its interpretations were often far from perfect. He therefore felt that one had to be conscious of their shortcomings. What is pertinent, however, is his view that although one must be aware of such faults, they should not encourage us to abandon the faith. Instead, it was essential to strive to overcome them and strengthen the faith. What he was saying in substance was that if one were born a Hindu, for instance, one must remain a Hindu and not opt for any other religion even while trying to remove such shortcomings that one felt Hinduism suffered from. In pursuance of this thought Gandhi made some interesting observations. He said:

> Even as a tree has a single trunk, but many branches and leaves, so there is one true and perfect Religion, but it becomes many, as it passes through the human medium. The one Religion is beyond all speech. Imperfect men put it into such language as they can command, and their words are interpreted by other men equally imperfect. Whose interpretation is to be held to be the right one? Everybody is right from his own standpoint, but it is not impossible that everybody is wrong. Hence the necessity for tolerance, which does not mean indifference towards one's own faith, but a more intelligent and purer love for it. Tolerance gives us spiritual insight, which is as far from fanaticism as the north pole from the south. True knowledge of religion breaks down the barriers between faith and faith.

Throughout his twenty-one years in South Africa, Gandhi had but one thought: endeavouring to realise God through service to humanity, confirmed in his belief that God was neither in heaven nor down below, but in every one. All that one needed to do in the circumstances was to let religion pervade every one of our actions. And that meant a belief in ordered moral government of the universe.

Gandhi held that man's ultimate aim should be the realisation of God, and consequently, that all his activities—political, social, and religious—had to be guided by the ultimate aim of the vision of God. But how was one to achieve that aim? Gandhi had a ready answer. The means to do that were simple enough if one recognised the unity of God and his creation. Therefore, if one identified God with all his creatures, serving humanity provided the answer. He thus advocated service of all.

That was more easily said than done. Whom did Gandhi mean when he said "service of all"? Whom did "all" include? On this issue Gandhi comes through very clearly. When he referred to all, for all practical purposes, he meant one's fellow countrymen. And this is how he explained what he meant:

> And this [service of all] cannot be done except through one's country. I am part and parcel of the whole and I cannot find Him apart from the rest of humanity. My countrymen are my nearest neighbours. They have become so helpless, so resourceless, so inert that I must concentrate on serving them. If I could persuade myself that I should find Him in a Himalayan cave, I would proceed there immediately. But I know that I cannot find Him apart from humanity.

So he returned to India from South Africa to find his "nearest neighbours" and to serve them. Thereby, he hoped, he would find God. It was all very well to serve people—and in India he served them beyond anybody's expectations—but Gandhi had something else on his mind, and that was prayer.

Gandhi had immense faith in prayer as a force. Prayer, he once revealed, even saved his life. Without it, he noted with amazing frankness, he should have been "a lunatic" a long time ago. There were times in his life when he had some bitter experiences, which had made him miserable and desolate for a while. He was to say that if he was able to get rid of that despair, it was because of prayer. Prayer had not been a part of his early life as truth had been. Prayer came to him "out of sheer necessity" as he found himself in a plight where he could not possibly be happy without it. He was quickly to learn that just as food was indispensable for the body, so was prayer indispensable for the soul. He went even further to assert that while starvation was often necessary to keep the body in good health, there was no such thing as "prayer starvation". One could not possibly have a surfeit of prayer. Gandhi said that three of the greatest teachers of the world—Buddha, Jesus, and Mohammed had left unimpeachable testimony that they found illumination through prayer and could not possibly live without it. As for Gandhi, it was an inalienable part of his life. As he put it:

> In spite of despair staring me in the face on the political horizon, I have never lost my peace. In fact I have found people who envy my peace. That peace, I tell you, comes from prayer. I am not a man of learning but I humbly claim to be a man of prayer.

That was being totally frank. Gandhi did not proclaim what form prayer should take, as long as it was prayer. He was indifferent to form. Everyone was a law unto himself where prayer was concerned. He did, however, advise following the path pointed out by seers and sages of yore. He believed that praying every day would reveal something meaningful and make life richer and more satisfying.

So deep was his belief and faith in an ever-present God that he was surer of his existence than of the fact that he was sitting with another individual in a room. He went further than that in asserting his faith. He said, "I can also testify that I may live without air and water but not without Him. You may pluck out my eyes, but that cannot kill me. But blast my belief in God, and I am dead. You may call it superstition, but I confess it is a superstition that I hug, even as I used to do the name of Rama in my childhood when there was any cause of danger or alarm." Amazing confession. An even more revealing assertion made by Gandhi was that, in a certain sense, God was the source of all action, when he said that "in a strictly scientific sense, God is at the bottom of both good and evil". As he put it, "He directs the assassin's dagger no less than the surgeon's knife."

To those who insist—and there are many who are sceptical about Gandhi's struggle to achieve spirituality—that Gandhi was more a politician than a saint, his statement on the subject of politics and religion would be an apt reply:

> For me, politics bereft of religion are absolute dirt, ever to be shunned. Politics concern nations and that which concerns the welfare of nations must be one of the concerns of man who is religiously inclined, in other words, a seeker after God and Truth. For me God and Truth are convertible terms, and if anyone told me that God was a God of untruth or a God of torture, I would decline to worship him. Therefore, in politics also, we have to establish the Kingdom of Heaven.

Reference has been made to the use of the word "satan" by Gandhi. In a sense Gandhi admitted to the presence of Satan when he added, "But for all that good and evil are, for human purposes, from each other distinct and incompatible, being symbolical of light and darkness, God and Satan." Gandhi had referred to Satan a couple of times in his writings in *Young India*. A Hindu reader took objection to it, insisting that in Hinduism there is no place for Satan, the Fallen Angel, the Tempter. The reader asked, "How is it, then, that you who are a Hindu, speak and write as if you believed in the real existence of the old one?" Gandhi's reply is interesting. He wrote:

> I do believe that there is room for Satan in Hinduism. The Biblical conception is neither new nor original. Satan is not a personality even in the Bible. Or he is as much a personality in the Bible as Ravana or the whole brood of the *asuras* is in Hinduism. I no more believe in a historical Ravana with ten heads and twenty arms than in a historical Satan. And even as

> Satan and his companions are fallen angels, so are Ravana and his companions fallen angels . . . If it be a crime to clothe evil passions and ennobling thoughts in personalities, it is a crime for which perhaps Hinduism is the most responsible.

This sounds like a somewhat angry response but what, apparently, Gandhi was trying to convey is that one should not identify religions with a specific concept. As Prof. Bhikhu Parekh noted in an address he delivered in London in 2006, for Gandhi, "a religion was not a sovereign system of authorization beliefs and practices which its adherents may violate only on pain of punishment, but a great cultural resource which belonged to all mankind". To Gandhi, God was also love as he made clear in a major statement, even when his own belief was the truth of God. What he said about truth and God demands repetition:

> I would say with those who say God is Love, God is Love. But deep down in me, I used to say that though God may be Love, God is Truth, above all. If it is possible for the human tongue to give the fullest description of God, I have come to the conclusion that for myself, God is Truth. But two years ago [in 1929] I went a step further and said that Truth is God. You will see the fine distinction between the two statements, viz. that God is Truth and Truth is God. And I came to the conclusion after a continuous and relentless search after Truth which began nearly fifty years ago. I then found that the nearest approach to Truth was through love. But I also found that love has many meanings in the English language at least and that human love in the sense of passion could become a degrading thing also. I found too, that love in the sense of Ahimsa had a limited number of votaries in the world. But I never found a double meaning in connection with truth and not even atheists had demurred to the necessity of power of truth. But in their passion for discovering truth the atheists have not hesitated to deny the very existence of God— from

their own point of view rightly. And it was because of this reasoning that I saw that rather than say that God is Truth I should say that Truth is God.

After his return to India, Gandhi was a guest of Gopala Krishna Gokhale in Calcutta. During his days in Calcutta (now Kolkata), Gandhi often spent time walking up and down its congested streets and went to most places on foot. On one occasion, he had a long interview with Babu Kalicharan Banerji, a Christian who was then taking a prominent part in the Congress. Kalicharan had spoken to Gandhi about Calcutta's famous Kali Temple and he was eager to see it out of what seemed natural curiosity more than any devotion. On the way, he saw a stream of sheep going to be sacrificed to Kali. Rows of beggars lined the lane leading to the Kali Temple. There were religious mendicants too—Gandhi has referred to them as mendicants rather than as beggars—but Gandhi was always opposed to giving alms to sturdy beggars. A crowd of them pursued him. One such man was seated on a verandah and asked Gandhi where he was going. When Gandhi told him that he was visiting the Kali Temple, there was silence. Gandhi asked the mendicant, "Do you regard this sacrifice as religion?"

Replied the mendicant, "Who would regard killing of animals as religion?"

"In that case," Gandhi said, "why don't you preach against it?"

Back came the answer, "That's not my business. Our business is to worship God."

Gandhi was not going to let go of the man so easily. He asked, "But could you not find any other place in which to worship God?"

The man replied, "All places are equally good for us. The people are like a flock of sheep, following where leaders lead them. It is no business of us, *sadhus*."

Gandhi decided that there was no point in pursuing the discussion any further. He went on to the temple, with his companion and guide. The sight that met his eyes shocked him. The blood of the slaughtered sheep, flowing in rivers, was unbearable to behold. It was a spectacle he was never to forget. That evening, Gandhi was to dine with some of his Bengali friends. He took the opportunity to speak to one of them about the cruel form of worship that he noticed at the Kali Temple. Pat came the answer, "The sheep don't feel anything. The noise and the drum beating there deaden all sensation of pain." That was an answer Gandhi found hard to swallow. He told his friend that if the sheep had speech they would tell a different tale. He also proclaimed that the cruel custom of animal slaughter ought to be stopped. Gandhi, at that point, thought of Buddha's humanism but he also realised that arguing with his friend on animal slaughter was beyond his capacity. In his autobiography he wrote:

> I hold today the same opinion as I held then. To my mind the life of a lamb is no less precious than that of a human being. I should be unwilling to take the life of a lamb for the sake of the human body. I hold that, the more helpless a creature, the more entitled it is to protection by man from the cruelty of man. But he who has not qualified himself for such service is unable to afford to it any protection. I must go through more self-purification and sacrifice, before I can hope to save these lambs from this unholy sacrifice. Today I think I must die pining for this self-purification and sacrifice. It is my constant prayer that there may be born on earth some great spirit, man or woman, fired with divine pity, who will deliver us from this heinous sin, save the lives of the innocent creatures, and purify

the temple. How it is that Bengal with all its knowledge, intelligence, sacrifice, and emotion tolerates this slaughter?

To Gandhi, the seeker after God, the concept of offering Kali the sacrifice of sheep was shocking beyond imagination. Determined to understand the Bengali mind he decided to see some outstanding Bengali leaders. But Maharshi Devendranath Tagore was not available for an interview. He tried to meet Swami Vivekananda and went expectantly to Belur Math only to be told that the Swami was at his Calcutta residence, lying ill, and could not be seen. But he managed to see Sister Nivedita. It is not clear what he discussed with her. Would he have discussed the concept of animal slaughter—sacrifice, if that is the right word—with her? One doesn't know. But clearly he failed to find much meeting ground in their conversation.

Then came one last experiment with visiting a temple, which Gandhi has recorded with some passion in his autobiography. He was returning from Calcutta to Bombay and decided to visit Benares (Varanasi), famous for its temples and the Ganga flowing close by, a dip in which was enough to wash away one's sins. On his arrival at Benares, he was surrounded by numerous Brahmins and he decided to stay with one of them, offering him no more than a rupee and four *annas* as *dakshina*. Then he went to the ghats to take a dip in the Ganga as tradition demanded. After the *pooja* was over at noon, Gandhi went to the famous Kashi Vishwanath Temple for *darshan*. Terrible was his disappointment.

When practising as a barrister in Bombay in 1891, Gandhi had occasion to attend a lecture on "Pilgrimage to Kashi" in the Prarthana Samaj hall. He was, in the circumstances, somewhat prepared for what he saw and for some measure of disappointment. "But," he was to write, "the actual disappointment was greater than I had bargained for."

Everything disturbed him. The approach to the Vishwanath Temple was through a narrow and slippery lane. Quiet there was none. The swarming flies and the noise made by the shopkeepers and pilgrims were intolerable. Wrote Gandhi:

> Where one expected an atmosphere of meditation and communion, it was conspicuous by its absence. One had to seek that atmosphere in oneself. I did observe devout sisters, who were absorbed in meditation, entirely unconscious of the environment. But for this the authorities of the temple could scarcely claim any credit.

Gandhi had sought peace and tranquillity at the temple as expected in a house of God. Great was his sorrow to find the holy precinct converted into a crass commercial market with no trace of serenity.

When he reached the temple, he was greeted at the entrance by a stinking mass of rotten flowers. He went near the *jnanavapi* (well of knowledge) and "searched for God but failed to find Him". Gandhi even found the surroundings of the *jnanavapi* dirty. He had no mind to give any *dakshina*. When he offered a pie (a rupee consists of sixteen *annas* and each *anna* of twelve pies, making a rupee equal to 192 pies) to the priest, he was driven away. Gandhi was to write: "If anyone doubts the infinite mercy of God, let him have a look at these sacred places. How much hypocrisy and irreligion does the Prince of Yogis suffer to be perpetrated in His holy name?"

If Gandhi hoped for some spiritual sustenance at Benares, he was to be totally disillusioned. After that he was to go to the holy city twice but did not—and could not—pay another visit to the Kashi Vishwanath Temple. In fact, there is no reported instance of Gandhi ever again visiting any temple. By then, also, he had come to be known as a Mahatma, and people, eager to have his *darshan*, would not allow him to have a *darshan* of the temple. Gandhi was sadly to note, "The woes of *Mahatmas* are known to *Mahatmas* alone."

That he wanted to have the *darshan* of Kashi Vishwanath itself is a conundrum. Gandhi did not believe in a personal God. When once he was asked whether he did or did not, his reply was, "I don't. I don't. I don't believe God to be a personal being in the sense that we are personal beings. I understand God to be universal law. God is the law as well as the law giver. The two are one."

He believed in non-dualism. Advaita. As he explained, "I believe in the essential unity of man and also of all that lives." As Gandhi saw it, God was not "personal" in the sense that he has human form or limitations or likes and dislikes. But God was "personal" in the sense that he was approachable to man, was in closest relation with him, and was the spirit dwelling in the innermost recesses of man's heart. In his book *Gandhi's View of Life*, Chandrashanker Shukla, a well known Gandhian, has noted that Gandhi, like Shankara, adopted the formula "neti, neti" (not this, not this) and yet, like Ramanuja, described God as perfect truth, perfect non-violence, perfect innocence—in fact, the perfection of all the virtues known to man.

Gandhi did not deny the existence of Rama and Krishna but he did not worship them. To him, Rama and Krishna were incarnations of God, synonymous with perfection. He once told a Christian audience that he believed in the Krishna of his own imagination who was identical with God and had not much to do with the historical Krishna about whom there was a mass of conflicting evidence.

Was Krishna a historical figure? Shukla quotes Radhakrishnan as saying, "There is ample evidence in favour of the historicity of Krishna. In the *Gita*, Krishna is identified with the Supreme Lord . . . He is not a hero who once trod the earth and has now left it, having spoken to His favourite friend and disciple, but is everywhere and in every one of us, as ready to speak to us now as He ever was to anyone else. He is not a bygone personality but the indwelling spirit, an object for our spiritual consciousness."

Was Gandhi, then, subscribing to the concept of *aham brahmasmi*—I am God? True, Gandhi believed that God was within everyone, but that is not the same as saying "I am God". Gandhi felt closer to Rama than to Krishna, and it was the name of Rama that he invoked when he was shot. But he felt closer, not to the Rama of Valmiki who treats him as a great hero, but to Tulsidas' Rama. In that work, as Gandhi's secretary Mahadev Desai was to point out, Rama emerges as an eternal source of inspiration.

For Gandhi, it was not a matter of choice between Rama and Krishna. The devotee—*bhakta*—in Gandhi wanted Rama; the philosopher in him took to Krishna. Gandhi, in fact, was a combination of the *rajayogi, dhyanayogi, karmayogi,* and the *bhaktiyogi*. Gandhi was the perfect fighter for truth and non-violence. He was the perfect meditator, the perfect man of action, and lastly, the perfect devotee. The word "perfect" is not loosely used. Gandhi never claimed to be perfect. But he sought perfection. Gandhi meditated with total single-mindedness on the ideal of the Gita. He explains the influence of the Gita on him thus:

> The last eighteen verses of the Second Chapter of the *Gita* give in a nutshell the secret of the art of living . . .
>
> [Those] verses of the Second Chapter have since been inscribed on the tablet of my heart. They contain for me all knowledge. The truths they teach me are the "eternal

verities". There is reasoning in them, but they represent realized knowledge.

I have since read many translations and many commentaries, have argued and reasoned to my heart's content, but the impression that the first reading gave me has never been effaced.

To Gandhi, these verses were the essence of the Gita. In this chapter, Krishna explains to Arjuna that when a person's intellect becomes steady and he gains complete equilibrium, he is said to have attained yoga. And Krishna expounds the ideal qualities that a person must possess to be able to live in wisdom. Arjuna, perplexed, asks Krishna how one can recognise such a person. Among other things, Krishna replies:

Yaa nishaa sarvabhutaanaam tasyaam jaagarti samyami
Yasyaam jaagrati bhutaani saa nishaa pashyato muneh
(Ch. II, *Shloka* 69)

(That which is night for all beings therein the man of self-restraint is wide awake. Where other beings keep awake, it is night for the sage contemplating God.)

Vihaaya kaamaanyah sarvaanpumaamoshcharati nihspruh
Nirmamo nirahamkaarah sa shaantimadhigachchati
(Ch. II, *Shloka* 71)

(He who gives up all desires and experiences all the sense objects without any attachment is the one who finally attains salvation.)

In his book *Gandhi, The Man*, Eknath Easwaran elucidates the qualities of a man who lives in wisdom in these lines:

He lives in wisdom
Who sees himself in all and all in him,
Whose love for the Lord of Love has consumed

Every selfish desire and sense-craving
Tormenting the heart. Not agitated
By grief, nor hankering after pleasure,
He lives free from lust and fear and anger.
Fettered no more by selfish attachments,
He is not elated by good fortune
Nor depressed by bad. Such is the seer. . . .

The disunited mind is far from wise;
How can it meditate? How be at peace?
When you know no peace, how can you know joy?
When you let your mind follow the siren
Call of the senses, they carry away
Your better judgment as a cyclone drives
A boat off the chartered course to its doom. . . .

He is forever free who has broken
Out of the ego-cage of *I* and *mine*
To be united with the Lord of Love.
This is the supreme state. Attain thou this
And pass from death to immortality.

Adds Easwaran: "These are the verses which summarize Gandhi's life. For more than fifty years he meditated on them morning and night and devoted all his effort to translating them, with the help of the mantram, into his daily action. They are the key to his self-transformation." Of what the Gita meant to him, Gandhi wrote:

The *Gita* has been a mother to me ever since I first become acquainted with it in 1889. I turn to it for guidance in every difficulty, and the desired guidance has always been forthcoming. But you must approach Mother *Gita* in all reverence, if you would benefit by her ministrations. One who rests his head on her peace-giving lap never experiences disappointments but enjoys bliss in perfection. This spiritual mother gives her devotee fresh knowledge, hope and power every moment of his life.

Once, an American journalist who had been closely studying Gandhi's work and life over the years, asked him with the curiosity of a newspaperman, "Mr. Gandhi, can you tell me the secret of your life in three words?" "Sure," replied Gandhi, no doubt quite amused, "renounce and enjoy!" He could well have expressed the teaching of the *Ishopanishad*: "The whole world is the garment of the Lord. Renounce it and receive it back as the gift of God."

What is spiritualism? One could define it as a method to attain man's ultimate goal: salvation or moksha. As Gandhi said, "If I have any passionate desire it is only to reach God, if possible, at a jump and to merge myself in Him." Easily said, but seldom achieved by mere mortals. It calls for great *tapasya*—spiritual striving. One has to be clean both inwardly and outwardly. One has to suppress one's ego totally. It involves many things: the least, bhakti, call it complete surrender to God, and karma, unceasing service to mankind. Indeed, to all living things. It calls for total dedication to truth and non-violence. Gandhi also considered chastity or *brahmacharya*, which involves suppressing or channelising the sex instinct to higher and purer purpose, a necessary ingredient of spiritualism. Of this last, he said, "We have to rein in the animal passion and change it into celestial passion."

Gandhi was, to some extent, a man of strong sexual urges. He had been striving for a state of purity from a very young age but it had been difficult for him to achieve. Hence all his struggle and conflict. He was, as we know, married when he was very young. He entertained a guilt complex where sex was concerned. Making love, to him, was practically equivalent to carnal lust—almost sinful. Why should having sex be considered a sin? Some of our ancient rishis were married and had children. Sex, besides, could be a form of bhakti in rising to heights of joy and ethereal happiness. But Gandhi slipped into a state of guilt-feeling because of circumstances beyond his control.

It happened thus. He was young, still a student. His wife was expecting a baby. They were living with Gandhi's parents. Time came when Gandhi's father fell seriously ill. He had to be taken care of round the clock. An uncle of Gandhi came home hearing about his brother's illness. The brothers were deeply attached to each other and the younger one would sit by the bedside of the older, always attentive to his every need. Gandhi, too, was very much alive to his duties and responsibilities and would also sit by his father's bedside, often giving him a massage. One night, at around 11:00 p.m., Gandhi's uncle offered to relieve him. Gandhi had been with his father for long and continuous hours and it came as quite a relief to be asked to retire and have some rest. Gandhi went straight to his bedroom. His young wife, Kasturba, was fast asleep. He woke her up and was making love to her when a servant knocked at the door. Gandhi started with alarm. He was told to come out at once as his father was "very ill". Father was ill enough. Gandhi did not have to be told that. But he sensed that "very ill" meant something more terrible. And so it was. He was told that his father was no more. It was all over. Gandhi expresses his remorse in his autobiography.

> I felt deeply ashamed and miserable. I ran to my father's room. I saw that, if animal passion had not blinded me, I should have been spared the torture of separation from my father

during his last moments. I should have been massaging him, and he would have died in my arms. But now it was my uncle who had had this privilege . . .

The shame . . . was this shame of my carnal desire even at the critical hour of my father's death, which demanded wakeful service. It is a blot I have never been able to efface or forget, and I have always thought that, although my devotion to my parents knew no bounds and I would have given up anything for it, yet it was weighed and found unpardonably wanting because my mind was at the same moment in the grip of lust. I have therefore always regarded myself as a lustful, though a faithful, husband. It took me long to get free from the shackles of lust, and I had to pass through many ordeals before I could overcome it.

What was even worse was that the child that was subsequently born did not live for more than three or four days. A shame-faced Gandhi was to write about it, saying, "Let all those who are married be warned by my example."

What was there lustful about wanting to make love to one's own wife? In the first place, Gandhi was young. He was still a student. In the second place he was obviously tired and wanted relief. He sought it in sex—a perfectly legitimate feeling. But for Gandhi it was not love but "carnal lust". He felt guilty, and that guilt accompanied him for years right up to the time he settled in South Africa with his wife and three children. He had been wedded to a monogamous ideal ever since his marriage, faithfulness being part of the love of truth. But he was getting restless. It was not that he wanted to opt out of marriage but to opt out of sex. He chanced to discuss this with a man he respected, Raychandbhai, who sounded sympathetic to Gandhi's new aim. Yet, Gandhi was not sure about himself. He asked himself whether his faithfulness only consisted in making his wife "the instrument" of his lust. As he saw it, as long as he was "the slave of lust" his faithfulness was worth nothing. Kasturba, however, was never the temptress. Gandhi felt that it should be easier for him to take the vow of *brahmacharya* if only he willed it. It was only his weak will or, as he put it, his "lustful attachment" that was the obstacle. In his case, while his spirit was willing, his flesh was weak, and even after his conscience had been roused in the matter, he failed twice. This was around 1906 when he was hardly thirty-seven, still a comparatively young age to swear by *brahmacharya*. On the one hand he realised that his motive to move into celibacy was more to do with having no more children than with attaining any kind of spiritual bliss. That was sound enough a motive. He therefore tried to stay away from his wife. They tried to sleep in separate beds. Often, he would retire to bed only after a hard day's work that left him totally exhausted. None of these efforts bore fruit immediately but according to him, the seeds of the final resolution of the problem lay in the cumulative effect of these strivings.

By then Gandhi had decided to offer his nursing services to the Natal Government at the time of the Boer war. It then became his conviction—that had nothing to do with spiritualism—that procreation and the consequent care of children were inconsistent with public service. He discussed the matter of taking a vow of celibacy with some of his colleagues who seemed sympathetic to the idea. In those early stages he did not share his thoughts with Kasturba, his wife, though she must have guessed that her husband was up to something when he asked for separate beds. Finally, he did consult her and learnt that she had no objection. Still, Gandhi had great difficulty in making the final resolve. He just did not have the necessary strength. He asked himself how he was to control his passion. The elimination of carnal relationship with one's wife seemed unnatural to Gandhi but reposing full faith in God, he took the vow. Twenty years later, looking back on the past, Gandhi wrote:

> As I look back upon the twenty years of the vow, I am filled with pleasure and wonderment. The more or less successful practice of self-control had been going on since 1901. But the freedom and joy that came to me after taking the vow had never been experienced before 1906. Before the vow I had been open to being overcome by temptation at any moment. Now the vow was a sure shield against temptation. The great potentiality of *brahmacharya* daily became more and more patent to me.

Gandhi was to say that he did not owe a study of the Shastras the knowledge that a perfect observance of *brahmacharya* means realisation of *Brahman* and that it slowly grew upon him with experience. He wrote extensively on the subject of *brahmacharya*. As he saw it, life without *brahmacharya* was "insipid and animal-like". And then was to dawn on him the truth that "a life of perfect continence in thought, speech and action is necessary for reaching spiritual perfection". But with it also came the realisation that the observance of the law of continence is extremely difficult and is impossible without a living faith in God, which is living truth.

With the passing of years, Gandhi's adherence to *brahmacharya* became a passion with him. He defined *brahmacharya* as "the way of life which leads us to Brahma (God)". *Brahman* pervades every being and could therefore be searched by diving into and realising the inner self. That realisation was impossible without complete control of the senses. *Brahmacharya*, therefore, Gandhi argued, meant control in thought, word, and action of all the senses at all times and in all places. A man or woman completely practicing *brahmacharya* was absolutely free from passion. Such a one therefore lived nigh unto God and was godlike.

What had started as a social necessity, in the end, turned out to be a spiritual aspiration. Gandhi began to argue that the straight way to cultivate *brahmacharya* was *Ramanama*, the recitation of Rama's name. To top it all, he wrote:

> From that day when I began *brahmacharya*, our freedom began. My wife became a free woman, free from my authority as her lord and master, and I became free from the slavery to my own appetite which she had to satisfy... The manner in which my *brahmacharya* came to me irresistibly drew me to woman as the mother of man. She became too sacred for sexual love. And so every woman at once became sister or daughter to me.

In what way did the practice of *brahmacharya* strengthen Gandhi? Was the energy gained from celibacy converted into energy of another kind? There is an interesting report of a talk that the American correspondent, Louis Fischer, had with Gandhi's secretary, Mahadev Desai, in June 1942.

"All these days," said Fischer, "I have been trying to fathom the source of Gandhi's great influence. I have come to the conclusion, tentatively, that the chief reason for that influence is Gandhi's passion."

"That is right," Desai said.

"What is the root of his passion?" queried Fischer.

"This passion," explained Desai, "is the sublimation of all the passions that flesh is heir to."

"Sex?"

"Sex and anger and personal ambition. Gandhi can admit that he is wrong. He can chastise himself. Gandhi is under his own control completely. That generates tremendous energy and passion within him."

Chandrashanker Shukla, another admirer of Gandhi, noted that Gandhi aimed at the sublimation of the sex urge into the creative power of a higher kind. In that sense the practice of celibacy surely helped in spiritual growth of a kind that Gandhi himself had under-estimated before he took his vow.

It is an odd co-incidence, though as Penderel Moon stated, a more appropriate one, that Gandhi took his vow of *brahmacharya* when he was about to embark on a long career of public service and political agitation.

It may perhaps be presumptuous to say that Gandhi's attitude towards women changed once he took a vow of celibacy and *brahmacharya*. During his long career as a politician and public worker, he simultaneously remained a journalist and made his views known through the papers he edited, starting with *Young India* and ending with *Harijan*. Of women in general, he wrote:

- Woman must cease to consider herself the object of man's lust. The remedy is more in her hands than man's.

- Of all the evils for which man has made himself responsible, none is so degrading, so shocking or so brutal as his abuse of the better half of humanity—to me, the female sex, not the weaker sex. It is the nobler of the two, for it is even today the embodiment of sacrifice, silent suffering, humility, faith and knowledge.

- If I were born a woman, I would rise in rebellion against any pretension on the part of man that woman is born to be his plaything. I have mentally become a woman in order to steal into her heart. I could not steal into my wife's heart until I decided to treat her differently than I used to, and so I restored to her all her right by dispossessing myself of all my so-called rights as her husband.

- Chastity is not a hot-house growth. It cannot be protected by the surrounding wall of the *purdah*. It must grow from within, and to be worth anything, it must be capable of withstanding every unsought temptation.

- To call woman the weaker sex is a libel; it is man's injustice to woman. If by strength is meant brute strength, then, indeed, is woman less brute than man. If by strength is meant moral power, then woman is immeasurably man's superior. Has she not greater intuition, is she not more self-sacrificing, has she not great powers of endurance, has she not greater courage? Without her man could not be. If non-violence is the law of our being, the future is with woman . . . Who can make a more effective appeal to the heart than woman?

- Women are special custodians of all that is pure and religious in life. Conservative by nature, if they are slow to shed superstitious habits, they are also slow to give up all that is pure and noble in life.

It is not that Gandhi was against marriage in order to remain celibate or to serve mankind more effectively. As he saw it, marriage confirms the right of union between two partners to the exclusion of all others, but it confirms no right upon one partner to demand obedience of the other to one's wish for union. But then he asked, what should be done when one partner on moral or other grounds cannot conform to the wishes of the other? His reply was, "Personally, if divorce was the only alternative, I should not hesitate to accept it, rather than interrupt my moral progress, assuming that I want to restrain myself on purely moral grounds."

The question arose when he heard from a "sister" who was a good worker and was anxious to remain celibate in order to serve better the country's cause, but who got married, having met the mate of her dreams. A doubt arose in her mind: Had she done something wrong and fallen from the high ideal which she had set for herself? Wrote Gandhi:

> I have tried to rid her mind of this delusion. It is no doubt an excellent thing for girls to remain unmarried for the sake of service, but the fact is that only one in a million is able to do so.
>
> Marriage is a natural thing in life and to consider it derogatory in any sense is wholly wrong. When one imagines any act a fall, it is difficult, however hard one tries, to raise oneself. The ideal is to look upon marriage as a sacrament and therefore to lead a life of self-restraint in the married estate. Marriage in Hinduism is one of the four *ashramas*. In fact, the other three are based on it. The duty of the above-mentioned and other sisters who think like her is, therefore, not to look down upon marriage but to give it its due place and make it the sacrament it is. If they exercise the necessary self-restraint, they will find growing within themselves a greater strength for service. She who wishes to serve will naturally choose a partner in life who is of the same mind, and their joint effort will be the country's gain.

But in regard to the matter of practising celibacy and *brahmacharya*, Gandhi had a further problem. In order to cultivate purity in thought, word, and deed, a good deal depended on restraining oneself in the matter of food. Having taken a vow of *brahmacharya* Gandhi found it necessary to impose greater restraints upon himself in the matter of food—and this from a strictly religious point of view. As he saw it, passion in man is generally co-existent with the hankering after the pleasure of the palate. If a man could not control his palate, one could hardly expect him to be able to control his passions. Ergo, no vow of *brahmacharya* would work for a glutton. So Gandhi began with a fruit diet but from the standpoint of restraint, he did not find much to choose between a fruit-diet and a diet of food grains. He observed that the same indulgence of taste was possible with the former as with the latter and even more when one got accustomed to it. Gandhi was thus in a dilemma. He tried to resolve it by attaching greater importance to fasting or having only one meal a day on holidays. And if there was some occasion for penance or the like, he gladly utilised it too for the purpose of fasting. He tried various experiments, like selecting first one food and then another, while at the same time restricting the amount he ate. But, as he said, "the relish was after me". If he gave up one food item and took another, the latter only made him relish it even more! So he had one option open to him. Fasting. Fasting, he found, "can help to curb animal passion" but only if it is undertaken with a view to self-restraint. Fasting was futile unless it was accompanied by an incessant longing for self-restraint. Based on this he came to the conclusion that although fasting was one of the methods of attaining self-restraint, its efficacy depended on a combination of physical and mental discipline. Without fasting of the mind, the exercise would be insincere and superficial.

As in the matter of sex and celibacy, so in the matter of food, Gandhi was very clear about what needed to be done. "Perfect health can be attained only by living in obedience to the laws of God and defying the powers of Satan. True happiness is impossible without true health, and true health is impossible without a rigid control of the palate. All the other senses will automatically come under control when the palate has been brought under control. And he who has conquered his senses has really conquered the whole world, and he becomes a part of God."

By and large, Gandhi was convinced that as an external aid to *brahmacharya*, fasting was as necessary as selection and restriction in diet. Fasting undertaken with a view to control of the senses, Gandhi conceded, was very helpful. Gandhi warned that *brahmacharya* could not be attained merely by physical abstinence. The true *brahmachari* shunned false restraints. He created his own fences, according to his limitations. "The first thing is to know what true *brahmacharya* is, then to realise its value, and lastly to try to cultivate this priceless virtue."

Brahmacharya was self-purification. Gandhi prescribed the spiritual weapon of self-purification, intangible as it seems, as the most potent means of revolutionising one's environment and loosening external shackles. It worked subtly and indivisibly. It was an intense process though it might often seem a weary and long-drawn one. To Gandhi, self-purification by whatever name was the straightest way to liberation, the surest and quickest, and no effort could be too great for it. What it required to attain perfect *brahmacharya* was faith—an unshakeable mountain-like faith that flinched from nothing.

Gandhi vouched for yet another approach to gain spirituality and that was silence. He wrote: "Experience has taught me that silence is a part of the spiritual discipline of a votary of truth. Proneness to exaggerate, to suppress or modify the truth, wittingly or unwittingly, is a natural weakness of man, and silence is necessary in order to surmount it. A man of few words will rarely be thoughtless in his speech; he will measure every word." In the years after he returned to India and was active practically round the clock and involved in so many matters, silence became absolutely essential to him, both physically and spiritually. "Originally," he wrote, "it was taken to relieve the sense of pressure. Then I wanted time for writing. After, however, I had practised it for some time I saw the spiritual value of it. It suddenly flashed across my mind that that was the time when I could best hold communion with God. And now I feel as though I was naturally built for silence."

Gandhi maintained that silence of the sewn-up lips is no silence. Forced silence was only tantamount to the absence of words. It was only when one had the ability to speak and yet refrained from speech that he could be said to be truly silent. For Gandhi, silence became a means for "the preservation of and sublimation of, the vitality that is responsible for the creation of life". That vitality, he found, was continuously and even unconsciously dissipated by evil or even rambling, disorderly, and unwanted thoughts. And since thought is the root of all speech and action, the quality of the latter corresponded to that of the former. Hence, perfectly controlled thought was itself power of the highest potency and became self-acting. If man was after the image of God, he had but to will a thing in the limited sphere allotted to him and it "becomes". Such power was impossible in one who dissipated his energy in any way whatsoever. Hence silence was the answer.

It would appear that the wonderful efficacy of silence which he first experienced was when he visited a Trappist monastery in South Africa. Of that experience he wrote:

> A beautiful place it was. Most of the inmates of that place were under a vow of silence. I inquired of the Father the motive of it and he said the motive is apparent. "We are frail human beings. We do not very often know what we say. If we want to listen to the still small voice that is always speaking within us, it will not be heard if we continually speak." I understood that precious lesson. I know the secret of silence.

But what about saying prayer? To Gandhi, prayer was for remembering God and for purifying the heart, and could be offered even when observing silence. "As I believe that silent prayer is often a mightier (force) than any overt act, in my helplessness I continuously pray in the faith that the prayer of a pure heart never goes unanswered."

For Gandhi there was a close link between silence and prayer. As a matter of fact, Gandhi has dealt with the subject in as much length as he has dealt with many other paths to God. In prayer, Gandhi never found him lacking in response. Indeed, Gandhi found him nearest at hand when the horizon seemed darkest, especially during his ordeals in jail when it was not all smooth sailing for him. Gandhi did not believe that prayers were superstition. He insisted that they were indeed "more real than the acts of eating, drinking, sitting or walking" and that he could not recall a moment in his life when he had a sense of desertion by God.

Gandhi did not have the slightest doubt that prayer was an unfailing means of cleansing the heart of passions but it had to be combined with the utmost humility. And, as he put it, "It is better in prayer to have a heart without words, than words without a heart." Did one need an image to say a prayer to? Gandhi did not think so. He did not disbelieve in idol worship; certainly an idol did not excite any feeling of veneration in him. But he conceded that idol worship was part of human nature. Man hankered after symbolism. Images were an aid to worship. He claimed that he was both an idolater and an iconoclast. He valued the spirit behind idol worship but he was opposed to the shape of fanaticism that refused to see any virtue in any other form of worshipping the deity save one's own. Gandhi clarified that the object of worship in a temple was not the stone idol but the God it represented. The idol was a physical manifestation of the divine force that the devotees invested it with, and independent of such investiture, it remained a powerless stone statue. Since such force was transmitted to the idol through the prayers of the devotees, it was necessary that everyone maintained perfect silence at prayer time.

Prayer, to Gandhi, was the first and the last lesson in learning the noble and brave act of sacrificing self in the various walks of life, culminating in the defence of the liberty and honour of one's nation. Undoubtedly, prayer required a living faith in God. Man often repeated the name of God mechanically and expected fruit from so doing. The true seeker, Gandhi held, must have that living faith which would not only dispel the untruth of perfunctory repetition from within him but also from the hearts of others. To Gandhi, prayer meant an invocation for the blessing of God and it was not the words but the attitude that mattered.

Gandhi was of the firm belief that a man may be able to do without food for a number of days, but, believing in God, man cannot, should not, live a moment without prayer. Gandhi said that he was aware of many, who, whether from mental laziness or from having fallen into a bad habit, believed that god *is*, and would help them unasked. Why, then, was it necessary to recite his name?

> It is true that if God is, He is, irrespective of our belief. But realization of god is infinitely more then mere belief. That can come only by constant practice . . . I agree that, if a man could practice the presence of God all the twenty four hours, there would be no need for a separate time for prayer. But most people find this impossible. The sordid everyday world is too much with them. For them the practice of complete withdrawal of mind from all outward things, even though it might be only for a few minutes everyday, will be found to be of infinite use. Silent communion will help them to experience the undisturbed peace in the midst of turmoil, to curb anger and cultivate patience.

> It should be the general rule that prayers must not be delayed for anybody on earth. God's time never stops. From the very beginning the wheel of His time has gone ceaselessly on. As a matter of fact, there is no beginning for Him or His time . . . How can anyone afford to miss the time of offering prayer to Him whose watch never stops?

Gandhi reminded his readers that in the first *shloka* of *Ishopanishad* that is repeated everyday, at the beginning of the prayer, one is asked to dedicate everything to God and then use it to the required extent. The principal condition laid down is that one must not covet what belonged to another. Those two maxims, Gandhi insisted, maintain the quintessence of Hindu religion.

True meditation consisted in closing the eyes and ears of the mind to all except the object of one's devotion. Hence the closing of eyes during prayers was an aid to such concentration. Wrote Gandhi: "He can truly pray who has the conviction that God is within him. He who has not, need not pray. God will not be offended, but I can say from experience that he who does not pray is certainly a loser."

As Gandhi saw it, it did not matter if one individual worshipped God as Person and another as Force. Both did right according to their lights. No one could say with authority which was the absolutely proper way to pray. But the ideal must always remain the ideal. One needed only to remember that God is the Force among all the forces. All other forces were material but God, Gandhi averred, was eternal, omnipotent, and omnipresent.

There is a touching reference to what Rev. Jesudasan called "Gandhian Christology". That, he explained, is an expression of liberation based on the spirituality of a liberator who is placed beside Jesus Christ, becomes another Christ, and does not replace or displace him. Writes Rev. Jesudasan: "Gandhi resolved the contradiction (between religious faith and process of social liberation) by making religious faith an ally and an instrument in the social and political liberation of human beings. Social and political liberation were correlatives to spiritual liberation." But even more important, he added: "In his unflinching dedication to truth as God, in his relentless attempt to realise the truth through action and prayer, in his openness to correction and criticism, in his alignment with the poor and the voiceless, and in his suffering and death for justice sealed in fellowship and reconciliation, Gandhi can be seen as a man of prayer with Francis of Assisi and Ignatius of Loyola, to be placed with Christ the Liberator." And he quoted quite aptly and contextually, the prayer of St. Francis:

> Lord, make me an instrument of thy peace;
> Where there is hatred, let me sow love;
> Where there is injury, pardon;
> Where there is doubt, faith;
> Where there is despair, hope;
> Where there is darkness, light;
> And where there is sadness, joy.
> O Divine Master, grant that I may
> Not so much seek to be consoled, as to console;
> To be understood, as to understand;
> To be loved, as to love;
> For it is I giving that we receive
> It is in pardoning that we are pardoned;
> And it is in dying that we are born to eternal life.

Gandhi, let it be clear, did not go to South Africa to learn how to be a saint. He went there to plead the case of a legal client, not to achieve Mahatmahood. True, there were within him the seeds of religiosity sown by circumstances over which he had no control. His family origins, his natural surroundings, his exposure to religion, the environmental openings, the presence of a domestic servant, Rambha, who instilled values in him, all together went to make Mohandas Gandhi the ultimate Mahatma. Some of the techniques he tried out in South Africa like satyagraha and non-violence were to be honed to perfection following his return to India. One wonders whether the man who was known as Mohandas and was born in Gujarat would have become a Mahatma had he been born, let us say, in Punjab or even in Tamil Nadu. What was there in his DNA that turned him towards God? Would Gandhi have become the Mahatma had things been different in South Africa? Or if he had lived in Great Britain?

As suggested by Penderel Moon in his biography of Gandhi, the eventual success of satyagraha in South Africa could well be attributed to providence. By 1912, the movement was on a definite decline and what it did achieve was largely owed to Gopala Krishna Gokhale's astute handling of it. In addition to that, the threat of a railway strike had intimidated the government into taking a mellower stance. Possibly. But his long stay in South Africa of over two decades had enabled him to practise some of the techniques that were to stand him in good stead in India, such as ahimsa, satyagraha, and *brahmacharya*. Were they mere techniques to be used to attain political goals under circumstances that made violence unproductive, or did they spring from the heart? Were they primarily Gandhi's modes to attain spirituality, which, at that point in time, seemed sensibly practical for attaining India's independence? One presumes that attaining spiritual bliss was as much in Gandhi's mind as attaining independence for India and that, if, somehow, the two aims got entangled, it was due "to the hand of God". In other words, the times proclaimed the man. Had Britain conceded independence to India, without India having had to fight for it, there would not have been a need for Gandhi even if one such existed. Such a man would probably have been spending his time either in a Himalayan cave, or like a Dayananda Saraswati or a Swami Vivekananda, moving around the country to address politically uncertain audiences. As things stood, the times were such in the first decade of the twentieth century in India, that India needed a man like Gandhi. If Gandhi did not exist, such a one would have had to be invented. There had been others in the political and socio-religious field, men like Sri Ramakrishna Paramhansa, Swami Vivekananda, Mahadev Govind Ranade, Gopala Krishna Gokhale, not to speak of Dayananda Saraswati and countless others but there had to be only one Gandhi. And Mohandas Karamchand Gandhi filled the bill. He could speak the Indian language of spiritualism and, at the same time, he could be leader of an unabashed Indian independence movement. No matter how lowly the West thought India and Indians, the latter could quickly grasp non-violence as a very useful weapon against the armed might of Great Britain. More than anyone in the Christian world, Indians could appreciate such concepts as ahimsa, *satya* and satyagraha, *tyaga* (sacrifice) dharma, *tapasya* (spiritual practice), *vairagya* (renunciation), without someone having to explain their meaning to them. They were familiar with *satyameva jayate* (truth always triumphs), *ahimsa paramo dharma* (non-violence is the highest morality), and concepts like that, instinctively. Gandhi had only to practise these laws to get ready disciples. These concepts were in the Indian blood; they were so much a part and parcel of their lives. All that they needed was someone to show them the way to practise them, and Gandhi became the man to do that. His personal desire to attain God beautifully coincided with the nation's desire to be liberated. The two blended with almost divine forethought in the life of Gandhi. It had been ordained that he should be a Mahatma.

India, at the beginning of the twentieth century, had hardly been under British rule for five decades. Prior to 1857, India was barely a politically united India. Culturally it may have been one. One spoke of Bharat as *asetu himachala paryanta*—from the bridges at Rameshwaram to the heights of the Himalayas. A

Shankaracharya could travel from Kanya Kumari to Badrinath, unchallenged, and establish his *mutt*s in the four corners of India. But politically, India was a fragmented land. The British, it needs to be remembered, brought peace to the country and, even more significantly, brought it unity. The telegraph lines made instant or quick communication possible. The railways made travel easier. And without, perhaps, their wishing to, the British instilled into the enslaved Indians, the desire for freedom. And because they were British, non-violent non-cooperation against them seemed possible. Whether that would have been possible if the white rulers in India had been the French, the Germans, or the Russians, is another matter. We know what happened to the Indians in Goa under the Portuguese and to the Vietnamese in Southeast Asia under the French. And as for Germany, Hitler is reported to have said that under Nazi rule a Gandhi would have been shot dead. Perfectly believable. Whether one cares to admit it or not, it is most likely that only under the British could a Gandhi have practised satyagraha and ahimsa without much hindrance, except periods of imprisonment. That he had attained a certain amount of proficiency in the practice of these virtues in South Africa may, for all we know, have been God-ordained. That it had become Gandhi's conviction that both ends and means must be based on truth and ahimsa was a self-discovery that cannot be attributed to conditions in South Africa. In his philosophy of life, means and ends were convertible terms. To Gandhi, means were everything. So were ends. To him *brahmacharya* was a means to a noble end of attaining spirituality. The two were inseparable. As Gandhi himself put it, there was no wall of separation between means and ends. Indeed, Gandhi was to say, ahimsa and truth are so intertwined that it is practically impossible to disentangle and separate them. Ahimsa was the means. Truth, the end. There were no violent shortcuts to success.

In this matter of ends and means Gandhi was quite clear in his mind as to how he should act. "However much I may sympathise with and admire worthy motives, I am an uncompromising opponent of violent methods even to serve the noblest of causes. There is, therefore, really no meeting-ground between the school of violence and myself."

A scholar, J. B. Kripalani, who was later to join the congress and become its president, when first he heard Gandhi talk about non-violence, had the courage to walk up to him and tell him point-blank, "Mr. Gandhi, you may know all about the Bible or the *Bhagavadgita*, but you know nothing at all about history. Never has a nation been able to free itself without violence." Gandhi took the verbal assault smilingly. He told the young Kripalani, "You know nothing about history. The first thing you have to learn about history is that because something has not taken place in the past does not mean that it cannot take place in the future."

In Gandhi's philosophy, wrong means never yielded right ends. One did not worship God through Satan. Gandhi was as concerned with preventing the brutalisation of human nature as with the prevention of the sufferings of his own people. It was his strong belief that people who voluntarily underwent a course of suffering raised themselves and the whole of humanity. And he was equally sure that people who became brutal in their desperate efforts to get victory over their opponents or to exploit weaker nations or weaker men not only dragged themselves down but mankind as well. For Gandhi, in the circumstances, the attainment of great ends could only be achieved by adoption of equally noble means.

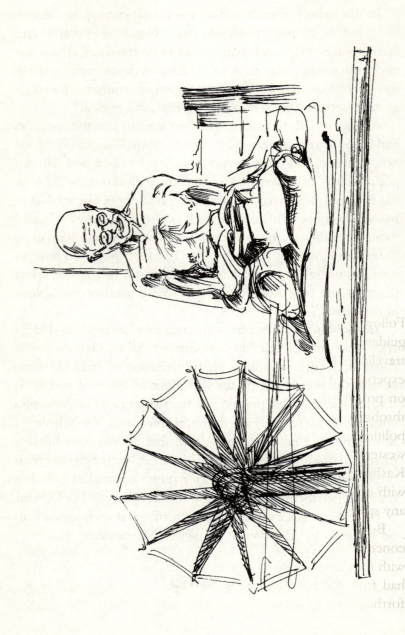

3

PATHS TO SPIRITUALITY

Following his return to India in 1915, Gandhi received political guidance from Gokhale who instructed him to spend a year travelling all over the country to gain knowledge and political experience. He also advised Gandhi not to express any opinion on political issues then plaguing the land. Not that India was throbbing with activity. The First World War had started and political life in India was at a low ebb. Gandhi had discarded his western clothes and wore only a dhoti, a shirt, and a cheap Kashmiri cap, and travelled third class. He could thus mingle with ordinary folk and hear about their woes without making any special effort or sounding inquisitive.

But even as he was going around the country, his main concern was to establish an ashram where he could settle down with the group of relations and co-workers from Phoenix who had followed him back to India. Help and cooperation were forthcoming. Gokhale himself was sympathetic and financially helpful. The ashram, founded in 1915 in Ahmedabad, was first located in a hired bungalow only to be shifted later to a site on the banks of the river Sabarmati. This new place was called Satyagraha Ashram though to many it was better known as Sabarmati Ashram. It had as inmates, forty men, women and children and it reflected Gandhi's desire to acquaint India with the method he had tried out in South Africa and to test the extent to which its application might be possible in India.

The Indian National Congress then was hardly a power to be reckoned with and was just about three decades old. Gandhi had yet to find his place in it. He had returned to India fervently hoping to work with Gokhale but he had hardly come home, when, within a few weeks of his landing in Bombay, Gokhale was no more. Gandhi felt orphaned. Not that Gokhale had always been in agreement with his disciple. Indeed, he had hoped that after a year's travel, Gandhi would find the need to change some of his views. Without Gokhale to guide him politically, Gandhi had to find his own path forward. An early instance of his success in leadership involved the removal of a customs cordon at Viramgam in Kathiawar that was causing considerable hardship to many. Gandhi saw Lord Willingdon, then governor of Bombay, who told him that if the matter was within the jurisdiction of his government the cordon would have been abolished long ago. So Gandhi did the next best thing. He approached the viceroy, Lord Chelmsford, no less, who was quick to oblige. The cordon was removed to the satisfaction of the people. The incident provoked an official of the Bombay Government to criticise Gandhi for threatening the government, pointing out that a powerful government was not one to yield to threats. Gandhi's reply was classical. He made it clear that far from threatening the powerful British government, he had been educating people in the ways they could lawfully overcome their problems. He reiterated that he did not believe in violence, which would normally result in such instances. Instead, he had been advocating the practice of satyagraha, which was a peaceful, non-violent method of protest.

This was just the beginning. Gandhi was ever alert to find issues that could be resolved through satyagraha. His attention was drawn to the issue of indentured labour. In this matter Gandhi could speak with authority for he knew what indentured labour had done to poor Indians seeking work in a white country. It was tantamount to semi-slavery. Gandhi appealed to the viceroy again. The viceroy's first reaction was to give a somewhat vague promise to abolish it. Gandhi arranged for meetings to be held in Bombay, Calcutta and other centres to press his case. It worked. And without actually having to resort to satyagraha, he won. The government announced the ending of the indentured system on time. It was one more feather in Gandhi's cap.

These two minor incidents in themselves were not very significant but they were a prelude to greater things to come, which pushed Gandhi onto the national stage and invited the attention of the public to a new source of leadership and a new way to fight injustice. Gandhi and satyagraha were becoming synonymous. Gandhi could not possibly have dreamt how things would turn out when, during the meeting of the Congress Party in Lucknow in 1916, a simple agriculturist caught hold of him and insisted on his visiting Bihar to see conditions for himself.

On that occasion, Gandhi had no concept of what the agriculturist was talking about. But the latter was persistent. He waylaid Gandhi first at Cawnpore and then again in Calcutta, requesting him to come and survey the situation in Bihar. Unable still to persuade Gandhi, the man came down all the way to Ahmedabad and to Sabarmati Ashram to unburden himself of his tale of woe.

The problem concerned the tenants of indigo planters in the distant northern district of Champaran, which reached right up to India's border with Nepal. The land belonged to rich and powerful landlords. The sufferers were their tenants. Under the then prevailing system, known as *tinkathia*, the tenants were bound by law to plant three-twentieth of their land with indigo. But that was not all. They were also liable to unlawful exactions and bullying by their masters—and therein lay all their heartaches. This was something entirely new to Gandhi. His first reaction was to record the statements of those who claimed to suffer from the landlords' tyranny, and if it became inevitable, invite police attention and subsequent court trial. But deep down Gandhi must have thought that the situation was ideal for the practice of satyagraha.

As usual, Gandhi went about his job with systematic discipline. First, he sought interviews with the secretary of the Planters' Association, and the commissioner of the Division, as became a man who respected the views of all concerned in a dispute. Not that it helped. As far as the secretary and the commissioner were concerned, he was a virtual interloper and the latter even went to the extent of advising Gandhi to leave the Division forthwith. Indeed, a day or two after Gandhi reached Motihari, headquarters of Champaran district, he was served with an order to leave the district on the grounds that his continuing presence might lead to disturbances. Gandhi, as was only to be expected, declined to leave. This led to a summons to appear before a magistrate the very next day to stand trial for disobeying a legal order.

An order from the court to appear before it was nothing new to Gandhi. He did as he was told and even pleaded guilty and read out to the magistrate a "dignified and cogent statement" as Penderel Moon put it delicately, explaining his reasons for coming to the district in the first place and for disobeying the order to leave it. No magistrate before had faced such a situation! The unhappy and puzzled man adjourned the case without passing judgement but before the date of the next hearing he informed Gandhi that the case against him had been withdrawn by order of the government. Even more significantly, the collector of the district wrote to Gandhi saying that he was quite at liberty to conduct his proposed enquiry, and what was more, could count on all help he needed from local officials. Gandhi could not have expected a better deal!

It was not just the magistrate or the collector who dismissed the case—a bogus one to begin with—against Gandhi's presence in Champaran. The intervention came all the way from instructions of the viceroy and the governor. Gandhi, furthermore, was to be placed on a governmental commission of inquiry into the Champaran farmers' grievances, which eventually were redressed though it took several months. But no matter. Justice was done. Gandhi was later to claim that it was "no exaggeration, but the literal truth, to say that in this meeting with the peasants, I was face to face with God, Ahimsa and Truth".

About this event, Charles F. Andrews, a very close friend of Gandhi who alone was known to address him by his name Mohan, writes:

> [In the case of Champaran] satyagraha had actually to be offered. Mere preparedness for it did not suffice, as powerful vested interests were arrayed in opposition. The peace maintained by the people of Champaran deserves to be placed on record. I can bear witness to the perfect non-violence of the leaders in thought, word and deed. Hence it was that this age-long abuse came to an end in six months.

The fourth struggle in which Gandhi engaged was that of the mill-hands of Ahmedabad against the mill-owners. By then

Gandhi had become well-known in Gujarat and could not possibly have been ignored. For example, following his success at Champaran, Gandhi was invited to become president of the Gujarat Sabha, a not particularly distinguished body that, as elsewhere in India, contented itself with passing resolutions and sending petitions to government whenever a seeming injustice took place. At about the same time, Vallabhbhai Patel, who was years later to be Gandhi's most loyal colleague, was elected secretary of that organisation. The story goes that Vallabhbhai was playing cards at his favourite club in Ahmedabad when he heard of Gandhi's victory at Champaran. It was to be the beginning of an era of close cooperation between the two till the day of Gandhi's assassination in 1948.

Gandhi had returned from Champaran when he was informed about the labour situation in Ahmedabad. The workers, in desperation, had asked for a thirty-five per cent raise in wages. Wages in Bombay had risen by fifty per cent but that was another matter. Ahmedabad was not Bombay. Gandhi told the workers, "You should address a letter to mill-owners about your grievances. We do not want any bitterness to grow between the two parties. We cannot all at once demand an increase of 50 to 60 per cent. We shall appeal to them with due firmness. If, despite that, they do not agree, we shall have five persons nominated by each side and accept their decision . . . With increased earnings as demanded by you, you should learn to be clean, should get rid of your various addictions and see that your children get education."

The workers were willing to listen to Gandhi's appeal for reasonable demands but the mill-owners were adamant. The situation worsened and it became clear that a strike by the workers was inevitable. The strike began on February 22, 1918. Gandhi's instructions to the workers were very strict. He wanted them to take a pledge as follows:

- Not to resume work until a thirty-five per cent increase in the wage was secured.

- Not to indulge, during the period of lock-out, in mischief, quarrelling, robbing, plundering, or abusive language, or cause damage to mill-owners' property, but to behave peacefully.

Every worker was asked to take the pledge with God as his witness. Throughout the period of the strike, Gandhi published pamphlets explaining what was happening day by day. He appealed to the mill-owners in the name of Jain or Vaishnava concepts of compassion. In India, he argued, pure justice was called "eastern or ancient justice". He said, "Out of feeling or regard, a father gives up many things for the son and vice versa, and in so doing, both eventually gain. In giving up for another, the giver experiences a feeling of pride and considers it a sign of his strength and not of weakness."

The mill-owners were clever. They offered the workers a twenty per cent rise, to induce them to return to work. It was a smart move but Gandhi saw through it. To keep the workers under control and not fall victim to the mill-owners' tactics, Gandhi offered to go on a hunger strike. When this was announced at a workers' meeting, the effect was electric. Mahadev Desai, Gandhi's secretary, was to write: "It requires a poet's pen to describe what happened." Tears were flowing down the eyes of everyone present. Hundreds of workers called on Gandhi to tell him: "We shall not falter even if the strike continues for months. We will give up the mills, do any work, and even beg, but we will not break our pledge."

The strike lasted twenty-two days but in the end the workers won their demands. Gandhi gave up his fast. In the last leaflet that Gandhi published on the subject he made a statement typical of him. He wrote:

> I must apologise to the employers. I have pained them very much. The oath to fast was taken to influence the workers; but everything in this world has two sides. So my oath had an effect on the employers also. I apologise to them humbly for this. I am as much their servant as the workers'.

In his book *Gandhi's Truth*, Prof. Erik Erikson has described the Ahmedabad strike as "The Event".

The next testing ground for satyagraha was Kheda, a district in Gujarat which was then in the grip of a famine. The year 1917-18 had been an exceptionally bad one for the villagers. Under the Land Revenue Rules, the cultivators could get full suspension for the year if the crop amounted to not more than twenty-five per cent of the normal yield. According to the farmers this was exactly what happened but the official tally would not accept the farmers' calculations. Farmers submitted their petitions and prayers to the Government but to no effect. Gandhi advised resorting to satyagraha—refusing to pay the dues and submitting to penalty. Government sought a compromise of sorts by granting full suspension of land revenues to one village and half-suspension to 103 villages. This was considered unfair and a fresh inquiry was sought. The Bombay government remained adamant and the peasants were threatened with immediate eviction unless they paid their rents in full. Gandhi called all the peasants and asked them to take a vow of passive resistance which said in part:

> We shall rather let our lands be forfeited than that by voluntary payment we should allow our case to be considered false or should compromise our self-respect. Should the Government, however, agree to suspend collection of the second instalment

of the assessment throughout the district, such amongst us as are in a position to pay will pay up the whole or the balance of the revenue that may be due. The reason why those who are able to pay still withhold payment is that, if they pay up, the poorer ryots may in a panic sell their chattels or incur debts to pay their dues, and thereby bring suffering upon themselves. In these circumstances we feel that, for the sake of the poor, it is the duty even of those who can afford to pay to withhold payment of their assessment.

The technique worked. In the end a compromise was reached without a fresh inquiry. The compromise, however, was not a real victory for Gandhi or satyagraha, since the government, not the people, was to decide who was poor and who was not. But the point is that for the first time in their history, the peasants were awakened to their strength, their capacity to suffer, and their ability to take their destiny in their own hands.

At this point, it is worthwhile to note what Gandhi thought of satyagraha and how he conceived it to be. He often spoke or wrote about it and what he said or wrote makes instructive wisdom.

• Satyagraha is a force that works silently and apparently slowly. In reality, there is no force in the world that is so direct or so swift in working.

• Satyagraha is gentle, it never wounds. Satyagraha must not be the result of anger or malice. It is never fussy, it is never impatient, and it is never vociferous. It is the direct opposite of compulsion. It is peaceful and it was conceived as a complete substitute for violence.

- Satyagraha is a relentless search for truth and a determination to reach truth.

- There can be no satyagraha in an unjust cause. Satyagraha in a just cause is vain, if the men espousing it are not determined and capable of fighting and suffering to the end; the slightest use of violence often defeats a just cause. Satyagraha excludes the use of violence in any shape or form, whether in thought, word or deed. Given a just cause, capacity for endless suffering and avoidance of violence, victory is a certainty.

- Since satyagraha is one of the most powerful methods of direct action, a satyagrahi exhausts all other means before he resorts to satyagraha.

- The conditions necessary for the success of satyagraha are: (1) The satyagrahi should not have any hatred in his heart for the opponent (2) The issue must be true and substantial and (3) the satyagrahi must be prepared to suffer for his cause.

- Satyagraha is utter self-effacement, greatest patience, brightest faith, and voluntarily suffering greatest humiliation. It is its own reward.

- Satyagraha literally means insistence on truth. This insistence arms the votary with matchless power.

- Satyagraha, to be genuine, may be offered against parents, one's wife or one's children, against rulers, against fellow citizens, even against the whole world.

- In satyagraha it is never the number that counts; it is always the quality, more so when the forces of violence are uppermost.

- It is never the intention of a satyagrahi to embarrass the wrong-doer. The appeal is never to his fear; it is, must be, always to his heart.

- The satyagrahi's object is to convert, not to coerce, the wrong-doer. He should avoid artificiality in all his doings. He acts naturally and from inward conviction.

- A satyagrahi must have a living faith in God for he is his only rock.

- A satyagrahi must believe in truth and non-violence as his creed and therefore have faith in the inherent goodness of human nature which he expects to evoke by his truth and love expressed through his suffering.

- A satyagrahi must lead a chaste life and be ready and willing for the sake of his cause to give up his life and his possessions.

- A satyagrahi must be a teetotaller and be free from the use of other intoxicants in order that his reason may be always unclouded and his mind constant.

- A satyagrahi must carry out with a willing heart all the rules of discipline as may be laid down from time to time.

- A satyagrahi should carry out the jail rules unless they are specially devised to hurt his self-respect.

- Satyagraha differs from passive resistance as the North Pole from the South. The latter has been conceived as a weapon of the weak and does not exclude the use of physical force or violence for the purpose of gaining one's end.

- Carried out to its utmost limit, satyagraha is independent of pecuniary or other material assistance.

- Although satyagraha can operate silently, it requires a certain amount of action on the part of the satyagrahi. For instance, he must first mobilise public opinion against the evil which he is out to eradicate by means of a wide and intensive agitation.

- The only weapon of the satyagrahi is God by whatsoever name one knows Him. Without Him, he is devoid of strength before an opponent armed with monstrous weapons.

- A satyagrahi bids goodbye to fear. He is, therefore, never afraid of trusting the opponent. Even if the opponent plays him false twenty times, the satyagrahi is ready to trust him the twenty first time, for an implicit trust in human nature is the very essence of his creed.

- The satyagrahi, whilst he is ever ready for a fight, must be equally ready for peace. He must welcome any honourable opportunity for peace.

- A satyagrahi never misses, can never miss, a chance of compromise on honourable terms, it being always assumed that in the event of failure, he is ever ready to offer battle. He needs no previous preparation; his cards are always on the table.

- There is no time limit for a satyagrahi nor is there a limit to his capacity for suffering. Hence there is no defeat in satyagraha.

- A satyagrahi has nothing to do with victory. He is sure of it but he has also to know that it comes from God. His is but to willingly suffer.

Gandhi's advice: satyagraha first and satyagraha last. There was no other or better road to freedom.

In many ways, satyagraha, to Gandhi, was just another way of attaining spirituality. He maintained that satyagraha was an attribute of the spirit within. He considered non-cooperation and civil disobedience as different branches of the same tree called satyagraha which was his *kalpadruma* (a tree supposed to grant all desires) and his *jam-i-jam* (universal provider). Gandhi, during his long years of spiritual search, considered satyagraha as part of his "search for truth" and to him truth was God. He went further in insisting that ahimsa (non-violence) was the light that revealed that truth to him. To that extent, then, the practice of ahimsa was another way to reach God.

As Gandhi put it, satyagraha never wounds. Writing in *Harijan* in 1933 he stressed this point:

> Satyagraha excludes every form of violence, direct or indirect, veiled or unveiled and whether in thought, word or deed. It is a breach of Satyagraha to wish ill to an opponent or to say a harsh word to him or of him with the intention of harming him. And often the evil thought or the evil word may, in terms of Satyagraha, be more dangerous than actual violence used in the heat of the moment and perhaps repented and forgotten the next moment. Satyagraha is gentle, it never wounds. It must not be the result of anger or malice . . . The reformer must have consciousness of the truth of his cause. He will not be impatient with the opponent; he will be impatient with himself. He must be prepared even to fast unto death. Not every one has the capacity or the right to do so. God is most exacting. He exacts humility from his votaries. Even fasts may take the form of coercion. But there is nothing in the world

that in human hands does not lend itself to abuse. The human being is a mixture of good and evil . . . but there is least likelihood of abuse when it is a matter of self-suffering.

Gandhi used to say that ahimsa and truth are so intertwined that it is practically impossible to disentangle and separate them. They were like two sides of a smooth metallic disc and nobody could tell the obverse from the reverse. Ahimsa was the means; truth was the end. To Gandhi, ahimsa was the bedrock of satyagraha, the "irreducible minimum" to which satyagraha adhered, and the final measure of its value.

In writing about Gandhi, the man, Eknath Easwaran recounts the story of an Indian monk in Vedic times, sitting on the bank of a river, praying silently. Nearby a scorpion fell from a tree into the river and the *sanyasi*, seeing it struggling in the water, bent over and pulled it out. He then placed the scorpion back in the tree where it belonged but even as he did so, the creature bit him on the hand.

Unmindful of that, the *sanyasi* went on with his silent prayers, *dhyana*, when the scorpion again fell into the river and, as before, the *sanyasi* thoughtfully picked it out to set it back on the tree and was again bitten. This little drama was repeated several times to the surprise and shock of a simple villager who was watching the scene. Perplexed by what he saw, he approached the *sanyasi* and reverentially said, "Swamiji, I have seen you saving that horrible scorpion several times and each time I saw it bite you. Why did you have to save it time and again?"

"Bhai," said the *sanyasi*, "the scorpion cannot help itself. It is his nature to bite."

"Agreed," said the villager, "but knowing that, why do you have to allow it to bite you?"

"Ah, Bhai," replied the *sanyasi*, "you see, biting is the scorpion's *swabhav*. Saving life is my *swabhav*. Neither of us can help being what we are!"

Gandhi believed that ahimsa should be man's *swabhav*. He said, "Non-violence is the law of our species as violence is the law of the brute. The spirit lies dormant in the brute and he knows no law but that of physical might. The dignity of man requires obedience to a higher law—to the strength of the spirit."

But Gandhi was no *sanyasi* in the sense the *sanyasi* in the story above was. As he said, he did not want to live at the cost of the life of a snake. He would let the snake bite him rather than kill the snake. But, he mused, if God put him to the test he might not have the courage to die, and the beast in him might seek to kill the snake in defending his perishable body.

Gandhi was aware of the fact that for most people non-violence was not a facile concept to understand or to practise. But he was convinced that if we prayed to God in all humility, constantly beseeching him to help us understand it, with a desire to act upon that understanding, we could come closer to practising it.

Gandhi continually reiterated the fact that non-violence did not mean weakness. Non-violence, as he understood it, was not passive or inactive. In one of his stronger articles he wrote that non-violence did not permit running away from danger leaving dear ones unprotected. It was the summit of bravery and was not meant for cowards or for those who were afraid to die. He was absolutely clear that he would prefer violence to cowardly flight and would not let a coward shelter behind so-called non-violence. His belief in the positive force of non-violence is summed up in his words: "There is hope for a violent man to be some day non-violent, but there is none for a coward." On another occasion he wrote: "No matter how weak a person is in body, if it is a shame to flee, he will stand his ground and die at his post. This would be non-violence and bravery. No matter how weak he is, he will use what strength he has in inflicting injury on his opponent, and die in the attempt. This is bravery, but not non-violence. If, when his duty is to face danger, he flees, it is cowardice. In the first case the man will have love and charity in him. In the second and third cases, there would be dislike or distrust and fear."

Lest he was misunderstood, Gandhi made it a point to say that strength did not come from physical capacity. It came from an indomitable will. He did not want to be known merely as a visionary. He claimed to be a "practical idealist". As he clarified, the religion of non-violence was not meant merely for the rishis and saints. It was meant for the common people as well since non-violence was the law of our species. And he added: "Non-violence in its dynamic condition means conscious suffering. It does not mean meek submission to the will of the evil-doer but it means putting on one's whole soul against the will of the tyrant. Working under this law of our being, it is possible for a single individual to defy the whole might of an unjust empire."

Cynics argued that Gandhi might well preach satyagraha and ahimsa but how were these concepts to be inculcated? Among many things, Gandhi suggested reliance on *brahmacharya*, which he described as one of the things eternal that count in the end. His concept of *brahmacharya* was total control over one's passions, both physically and mentally. Since all physical action arises from the mind, it is essential to first rein in thought, which, in turn, easily facilitates physical continence. As Gandhi saw it, one who attained perfect *brahmacharya* did not stand in need of protecting walls. But the aspirant for *brahmacharya* undoubtedly needed them "even as a young mango plant has need of a strong fence around it". Gandhi conceded that *brahmacharya* was not a virtue that could be cultivated by outward restraints. He who ran away from a necessary contact with a woman did not understand the full meaning of *brahmacharya*. The true *brahmachari* shunned all false restraints. He created his own fences according to his limitations, breaking them down when he felt that they were unnecessary. The first thing to know was what true *brahmacharya* was, then to realise its value, and only then to cultivate that priceless virtue.

Brahmacharya was such only if it persisted under all conditions and in the face of all possible temptations. A *brahmachari* was one who behaved like a marble statue unresponsive to all physical temptations. But just as a marble statue refrained from using its eyes or ears, even so should a man avoid every occasion of sin. Well said, but was that always possible? As a guideline in the quest for God-realisation, *brahmacharya* might be a useful means, but did Gandhi himself follow his own guideline? An English Christian correspondent once challenged Gandhi in this regard:

> You have had your name blazoned abroad . . . one of the greatest philosophers and sacrificial workers on earth. In India you have been proclaimed the Mahatma, and actually worshipped as one of the incarnations of India's many deities . . . your practice also of fasting when sin is committed . . . is a tendency to make Indians believe that you can merit blessing which can be communicated to others—but has anybody been loving and courageous enough to write and challenge you as to how, personally, you are going to attain atonement for your own sin? All your self-denials and fasting and prayer and good deeds cannot blot out one sin of your early days. For thirty or more years of your life, you lived the carnal, self-life, seeking and following your own plans and ambitions without seeking to know God's purpose for your life or to honour His holy name.

Gandhi answered in his typical style, in a manifestation of humility characteristic of authentic contact with God, at a level deeper than that exhibited by his overly zealous correspondent. He wrote:

> Jesus atoned for the sins of those who accepted his teachings by being an infallible example to them. But the example was worth nothing to those who never troubled to change their lives. A regenerate outgrows the original alloy. I have made the frankest admissions of my sins. But I do not carry their burden on my shoulders. If I am journeying Godward, as I feel I am, it is safe with me. For I feel the warmth of the sunshine of His presence. My austerities, fasting and prayers are, I know, of no value if I rely upon them for reforming me. But they have an inestimable value, if they represent, as I hope they do, the yearnings of a soul striving to lay his weary head in the lap of his Maker.

Gandhi had a high regard for fasting as a process of self-purification. He considered it a potent weapon in the satyagraha armoury except that he did not consider mere physical capacity to undergo it as any qualification for taking recourse to it. As an external aid to *brahmacharya*, Gandhi averred, fasting was as necessary as selection and restriction in diet. So overpowering were the senses that they could be kept under control only when they were completely hedged in on all sides from above and beneath. It was common knowledge that the senses were powerless without food and so fasting undertaken with a view to control of the senses was very helpful. With some, fasting was of no avail because assuming that mechanical fasting alone would make them immune they kept their bodies without food but feasted their minds upon all sorts of delicacies thinking all the while what they would eat and what they would drink after they terminated the fast. Such fasting, Gandhi warned, helped in controlling neither palate nor lust. Fasting was useful when mind cooperated with starving body, cultivating distaste for the objects that were denied to the body. Fasting, to Gandhi, was the complete denial of self; a means to self-purification. Mind was the root of all sensuality. Fasting, therefore, was of limited use, for a fasting man may continue to be swayed by passion.

As in all other matters, Gandhi defined his various conceptions towards a journey to God in clear and precise terms. Thus, in the matter of fasting, he said, "There can be no room for selfishness, anger, lack of faith or impatience in a pure fast ... Infinite patience, firm resolve, single-mindedness of purpose, perfect calm and no anger must of necessity be there. But since it is impossible for a person to develop all these qualities all at once, no one who has not devoted himself to following the laws of ahimsa should undertake a *satyagrahi* fast." Gandhi conceded that it cannot be denied that fasts can also be coercive. There were fasts to attain a selfish object. A fast, for example, undertaken to wring money from a person or for fulfilling some such personal end, would amount to the exercise of coercion or undue influence.

Was it possible to observe *brahmacharya* in its totality as demanded by Gandhi? He had strong views on the subject. He once wrote that he had known the writings and theories on sex by eminent writers like Havelock Ellis and Bertrand Russell. He conceded that they were all thinkers of eminence, integrity, and experience. He also reminded his readers that "they have suffered for their convictions and for giving expression to the same". He pointed out that while totally repudiating institutions like marriage, and the then current code of conduct, on which he disagreed with them, they were still firm believers "in the possibility and desirability of purity in life independent of those institutions and usages". He further noted that he had come across men and women in the West who led a pure life although they did not accept or observe current usages and social conventions. His own research ran somewhat in that direction:

If you admit the necessity and desirability of reform, of discarding the old, wherever necessary, and building a new system of ethics and morals suited to the present age, then the question of seeking the permission of others or convincing them does not arise. A reformer cannot afford to wait till others are converted; he must take the lead and venture forth alone even in the teeth of universal opposition. I want to test, enlarge and revise the current definition of *brahmacharya* . . . in the light of my observation, study and experience. Therefore, whenever an opportunity presents itself, I do not evade it or run away from it. On the contrary, I deem it my duty, my dharma to meet it squarely in the face and find out where it leads to and where I stand. To avoid the contact of a woman or to run away from it out of fear, I regard as unbecoming of an aspirant after true *brahmacharya*. I have never tried to cultivate or seek sex contact for carnal satisfaction. I do not claim to have completely eradicated the sex feeling in me. But it is my claim that I can keep it under control.

In the pursuit of testing his own *brahmacharya*, Gandhi slept in the naked with a few ashramites, and, of course, admitted to it in his columns in *Harijan*. He might have succeeded in showing that he could still control his passions but what his experiment did for his female partners has never been recorded. One of the most painful such "experiments" was during his last days in Naokhali in 1946 when communalism was literally running riot. The women he slept with have long been forgotten and are not known to have kept a record of *their* feelings, desires, and anxieties. Many of Gandhi's disciples, followers, colleagues, and fans were intensely disappointed, among them Vallabhbhai Patel and Vinoba Bhave, to name some of the best and brightest. But that is another story. When one is in one's twilight years there is no need to test one's *brahmacharya*. Why Gandhi should seek to test his power of practising *brahmacharya* in his late seventies remains a mystery for all the explanations Gandhi has given in his many writings.

The one explanation available—and even this can be disputed—is his total abhorrence of sex. He thought of it primarily as sinful. He frequently dismissed it as "animal instinct" or "carnal lust" and therefore unbecoming of any human being aspiring to attain God or moksha. He thought of sex as something unbecoming of men and women unless it was used strictly for getting progeny. If Gandhi had his way he would prevent any adult, even if married, from having sex with the use of a condom. He wrote extensively on the subject:

> The whole train of thought which underlines birth control is *erroneous* and *dangerous*. Its supporters claim that a man has not only the right but it is his duty to satisfy the *animal instinct* and that his development would be arrested if he did not discharge this duty. I think this claim is false. It is idle to expect self-restraint from one who takes to artificial methods. In fact, birth control is advocated on the ground that restraint of *animal passion* is impossibility. To say that such restraint is impossible or unnecessary or harmful is *the negation of all religion. For the whole superstructure of religion rests on the foundations of self-control.* (emphasis added)

We know what Gandhi has to say about sex, birth control, and sex control, but is the exercise and expression of desire a hurdle to the attainment of God? Is sex a sin that is unforgivable and does it keep God away from man? Can't a happy couple, fully at peace with each other after sex, be at peace with God as well? Sex is a natural instinct, like hunger. Is that to be denied to all true seekers after God? Is God so vicious that he will frown upon any man or woman who wants to have joy with a willing and equally relaxed partner? These questions may arise in the hearts and minds of many honest and god-fearing people but Gandhi was, as always, steadfast in his views. He reiterated his views on birth control thus:

> I want to revert to the subject of birth control by contraceptives. It is dinned into one's ears that the *gratification* of the sex urge is a solemn obligation like the obligation of discharging debts lawfully incurred and that not to do so would involve the penalty of intellectual decay. This sex urge has been isolated from the desire for progeny and it is said by the protagonists of the use of contraceptives that the conception is an accident to be prevented except when the parties desire to have children. I venture to suggest that this is a most dangerous doctrine to preach anywhere, much more so in a country like India where the middle class population has become *imbecile* through abuse of the creative function. (emphasis added)

Such has been Gandhi's revulsion of sex, that he would use words like "animal instinct", "animal passion" and "gratification" with complete abandon. There is no doubt that he detested sex but the larger question remains why, in his venerable old age, he should seek to test his *brahmacharya* by sleeping nude in bed with a woman perhaps half his age. Gandhi, of course, had his own answer. He wrote:

> My mind is made up. On the lonesome way of God on which I have set out, I need no earthly companion. Let those who will, therefore denounce me, if I am the imposter they imagine me to be, though they may not say so in so many words. I might disillusion millions who persist in regarding me as a Mahatma. I must confess, the prospect of being so debunked greatly pleases me.

Unfortunately, that is no answer to anyone truly seeking God. Is *brahmacharya* the only way of gaining spiritual deliverance? Is sex meant only for getting progeny? In what way were Laxmi and Saraswati related to Vishnu, or Parvati to Shiva? Or for that matter Rukmini (forget Radha for the moment) to Krishna, or Sita to Rama? Gandhi has no convincing answer. *Brahmacharya* may be one of the means of attaining spiritual salvation but it is surely not meant for everyone.

Closely associated with *brahmacharya* is another virtue: self-discipline. Indeed *brahmacharya* and self-discipline are closely connected and inter-related. Without self-discipline, there cannot be *brahmacharya* and *brahmacharya* is self-discipline of the highest order.

Brahmacharya, according to Gandhi, is inherent in Hindu civilisation and lacking in western civilisation. In any event, no western value has ever spoken about *brahmacharya*, *grihasthashrama*, *venaprastha*, and *sanyasa*. These are purely Hindu concepts that don't exist in the monotheistic religions like Christianity, Zoroastrianism, or Islam, nor were they part of the great civilisations of Egypt, Babylon, and Greece, great civilisations in themselves, but which, in due course, perished. According to Gandhi, "the reason for that was Indian civilisation has what they had not, *brahmacharya*."

That may not be totally accurate an assessment but it is true that India's essential spiritualism has lasted these thousands of years and has sustained the country through good times and bad. And this Gandhi attributed to "strict preliminary discipline which is necessary to qualify a person to make experiments in the spiritual realm". Indeed, as he put it, strict preliminary discipline was as necessary to enter the spiritual realm as "an indispensable scientific course of instruction is necessary just for conducting scientific experiments". Self-discipline was essential to be able to control the mind, which directs all actions.

Self-discipline also included abstemiousness from intoxicating drinks and drugs and from all kinds of foods, especially meat. This abstinence was undoubtedly a great aid to the evolution of the spirit though Gandhi was careful to point out that it was only one of the means to the end. As he explained, many a man eating meat and living in the fear of God is nearer his freedom than a man religiously abstaining from meat and many other things, but blaspheming God in every one of his acts. Gandhi's experience was that a vegetarian diet was best suited to those who wished to exercise self-control. He also strongly believed that diet played a crucial role in dictating the nature of an individual. He advocated a balanced approach to it, avoiding the extremes of overindulgence in food or measuring religious conduct in terms of diet.

All power, as Gandhi saw it, came from the preservation and sublimation of the vitality that is responsible for the creation of life. This vitality was continuously, and even unconsciously, dissipated by evil or by rambling, disorderly, and unwanted thoughts. And since thought is the root of all speech and action, the quality of the latter corresponded to that of the former. Hence, perfectly controlled thought in itself was power of the highest potency and became self-acting. Stating this in clear terms, Gandhi said, "If a man is after the image of God, He has but to will a thing in the limited sphere allotted to him and it becomes. Such power is impossible in one who dissipates his energy in any way whatsoever." But to that noble thought Gandhi added a corollary: "It is better to enjoy through the body than to be enjoying the thought of it. It is good to disapprove of sensual desires as soon as they arise in the mind and try to keep them down; but if, for want of physical enjoyment, the mind wallows in thoughts of enjoyment, then it is legitimate to satisfy the hunger of the body. About this I have no doubt."

But there was yet another corollary, which is sex-specific. Notes Gandhi: "Sex urge is a fine and noble thing. There is nothing to be ashamed of in it. But it is meant only for the act of creation. *Any other use of it is a sin against God and humanity.*" (emphasis added). Gandhi never considered himself to be an ascetic though. He describes his life as a strict, conscious effort towards evolution in the realm of the spirit.

> It is wrong to call me an ascetic. The ideals that regulate my life are presented for acceptance by mankind in general. I have arrived at them by gradual evolution. Every step was thought out, well-considered and taken with the greatest deliberation. Both my continence and non-violence were derived from personal experience and became necessary in response to the calls of public duty. The isolated life I had to lead in South Africa whether as a householder, legal practitioner, social reformer or politician required, for the due fulfilment of these duties, the strictest regulation of sexual life and a rigid practice of non-violence and truth in human relations, whether with my own countrymen or with the Europeans. I claim to be no more than an average man with less than average ability. Nor can I claim any special merit for such non-violence or continence as I have been able to reach with laborious research.

Self-discipline, to Gandhi, also involved self-purification. To him, the spiritual weapon of self-purification, intangible as it seems, was the most potent means of revolutionising one's environment and loosening external shackles. He believed that to attain perfect purity one had to free oneself of passion in thought, speech, and action. As he put it, "It is an intense process though it might often seem a weary and long-drawn process; it is the straightest way to liberation, the surest and quickest, and no effort can be too great for it. What it requires is faith—an unshakeable mountain-like faith that flinches from nothing."

Gandhi wrote extensively on this subject of self-purification. He held that identification with everything that lived was impossible without self-purification. Importantly, without self-purification, the observance of the law of ahimsa would remain an empty dream. And God could never be realised by one who was not pure of heart. Self-purification, therefore, must mean purification in all walks of life. And purification being highly infectious, purification of oneself necessarily led to the purification of one's surroundings. But Gandhi knew that all that was more easily said than realised.

> But the path of self-purification is hard and steep. To attain to perfect purity one has to become absolutely passion-free in thought, speech and action; to rise above the opposing currents of love and hatred, attachment and repulsion. I know that I have not in me as yet that triple purity, in spite of constant, ceaseless striving for it. That is why the world's praise fails to move me; indeed it very often stings me. To conquer the subtle passions seems to me to be far harder than the physical conquest of the world by the force of arms.

There is a beautiful and touching story, narrated by Eknath Easwaran, of how Gandhi put into practice both his concept of ahimsa and self-discipline. One evening, at the Sevagram Ashram, hundreds of people had gathered for the nightly prayer meeting. The sun was about to set and it was the time when snakes would come out of their holes after the fierce heat of the Indian day. That particular evening, those sitting in the front rows saw to their shock, a cobra, swiftly moving towards where Gandhi sat cross-legged. A ripple of panic began to sweep through the crowd as word went around and there was danger that there might be a stampede if the terror spread. But Gandhi sat immoveable, like a statue, covered only by his loin cloth, his legs, chest, and arms bare. While the crowd held its collective breath and watched in utter horror, the cobra made its way straight for Gandhi and slowly began to crawl up over his exposed thighs.

There was a long moment of silence in which no one dared to make a sound or move. Gandhi was heard quietly repeating God's name: "He Rama, Rama, Rama . . ." All that the crowd next saw was the cobra uncoiling itself and leaving the ground without hurting anyone, least of all Gandhi himself. It was an illustration not only of Gandhi's infinite faith in God, but in more immediate terms, his self-discipline. The slightest movement on his part may have served to rouse the cobra enough to bite him. And that would surely have been his end. Gandhi had often said, "For a non-violent person, the whole world is one family. He will thus fear none, nor will others fear him." What held good for human beings held good for a cobra as well! On yet another occasion Gandhi said, "Ahimsa is the attribute of the soul and therefore, to be practised by everybody in all the affairs of life. If it cannot be practised in all departments, it has no practical value." On that day, when the cobra coiled itself around him, he showed that he practised what he preached.

Gandhi's faith was an active one. It was not merely cognitive or contemplative. Action was as important as faith. In other words, he was a practitioner of what one might describe as *karma yoga*. With Gandhi, his precept and practice merged. Writing to a friend, Gangaben Vaidya, in May 1930, he said, "I keep myself busy and do not remain unoccupied even for a minute. That way alone can I have peace of mind. I can see God *only* through work. The Lord says that He is ever working without taking a moment's rest. How else can we know Him except through work?"

It is an interesting observation. Could Gandhi see God *only* through work? Could he not see him through truth or non-violence or self-purification or *brahmacharya*? Or for that matter through ahimsa? It is not that Gandhi was self-contradictory. One suspects that he saw God at different times in different ways and that all these ways merged into, and found expression through, his work. Once, while discussing the Gita, Gandhi sought to throw light on the nature of the work associated with faith. He identified such action with *yajna* (sacrifice) and interpreted it as "any work dedicated to God". In his letter to Gangaben he went a step further to say that when he spoke of work it was not mental or intellectual work that he had in mind but physical work. "Brahma did not ask human beings to multiply and prosper merely by working with their minds. What he meant was that they should do so through bodily *yajna*, by working with the body."

Gandhi's experiments with *brahmacharya* have been studied in great detail by Girja Kumar in his work *Brahmacharya Gandhi & His Women Associates* and by Prof. Bhikhu Parekh in his *Colonialism, Tradition and Reform: An Analysis of Gandhi's Political Discourse*. In his approach, respectful of Gandhi, the person, Girja Kumar nevertheless dares to reveal what was long known in Gandhi's immediate circle. His central thesis is as follows:

> What is remarkable about the Mahatma is not so much the thesis—many, before and after him, have found virtue in abstinence—but his extraordinary efforts to obtain this ideal, efforts that, inevitably perhaps, produced contradictions, affected the lives of his closest associates and produced a vision—a passionless society—that looks curiously naïve and not a little discomfiting, when compared with his still-inspiring political programme.

And Girja Kumar asks, "Did the man who led a movement that brought political freedom for so many go wrong on the issue of personal freedom?"

In the pursuit of his concept of *brahmacharya* he brought a great deal of unhappiness to many. Thus:

• Prabhavati, the wife of the distinguished socialist leader Jayaprakash Narayan, was a *brahmacharini* all her life. She was the subject of discord between Gandhi and J.P. She was torn between two loyalties but preferred Gandhi over her husband.

• Gandhi had an elaborate daily massage performed by young women. The massage was followed by a bath with the presence of a woman attendant almost essential.

• The further step on the road was the ritual of young women sleeping next to him, close to him, or with him. What started as a mere sleeping arrangement became, over time, an exercise to obtain the nirvana state of perfect *brahmacharya*. Gandhi was brutally truthful about his "experiment".

• Kanu Gandhi was upset because his wife Abha and his sister-in-law Vina Patel were most reluctant participants in the experiment. Gandhi's most intimate functions were not performed in privacy. Thus, he had his massage practically naked with young girls as his masseuses.

Gandhi's idealism, according to Girja Kumar, was not shared by the tallest among his associates like Kishorelal Mashruwala, Narahari Parekh, Kakasaheb Kalelkar, and Swami Anand.

By 1947, Gandhi was a lonely soul left to his resources. Writes Girja Kumar: "He was cheating himself without realising it, and all for the cause of *brahmacharya*. A stage came when he was all but disowned by his closest associates. Nirmal Kumar Bose had watched Gandhi from close quarters during his sojourn in Naokhali (1946-47). He had no hesitation in being critical of Gandhi and wrote to him: "I feel it is subordinating a human being to a purpose not determined independently by the person concerned." Gandhi's concept of *brahmacharya* found no favour with Vinoba Bhave who put forward the argument that any consciousness of difference between the sexes was "contrary to the ideal of *brahmacharya*". In other words, for any true *brahmachari* to be conscious of different sexes was a total violation of the theory and practice of *brahmacharya*. Convinced that Gandhi was beyond redemption, Vinoba decided to close any further discussion on the matter. As Vinoba saw it, if Gandhi were a perfect *brahmachari*, then he need not test his *brahmacharya*. If he were an imperfect *brahmachari*, then he should not take undue risks by testing it.

Meanwhile, there was practically a revolt in Gandhi's ashram. His son, Devdas, wrote a letter of strong protest to his father but Gandhi ignored it. Sardar Vallabhbhai Patel was furious. He spoke openly about Bapu indulging in *adharma* by his practice of sleeping with women without clothes.

Analysing Gandhi's experiments with sexual abstinence in *Colonialism, Tradition and Reform: An Analysis of Gandhi's Political Discourse*, Prof. Bhikhu Parekh writes:

> His thought during this intensely agonising period reveals a tendency latent in his earlier years but not fully manifest until now. He was determined to control the violence raging all around him. He was convinced that, as a national leader, he must accept responsibility for it. He was also convinced that all violence ceased in the presence of non-violence. He, therefore, concluded that if only he could eliminate all traces of violence and aggression within himself, he would be able to exert a quiet and "contagious" force and send out vibrations that would conquer the violence of his countrymen. Accordingly, he turned his attention inward and probed his psyche. He seems to have concluded that though he had

eliminated all traces of violence within himself, one still remained. . . . He associated sexuality with violence and aggression. So long as he was conscious of himself as a male, elements of aggression and violence were bound to remain, even if he was not conscious of them. The only way out was to cease to be a male, to become a woman. His final sexual experiment with Manu was an attempt to become, and to test that he had succeeded in becoming, a woman. This was why he said that he wanted to become a "mother" to Manu. This was also why, unlike his earlier experiments, he now asked her to keep a diary and show it to him every day. He was convinced that if he had really become a woman, she could not feel sexually stimulated in his presence, and wanted to be sure that that was how she felt . . .

Gandhi's experiment also linked up with another powerful strand in the Hindu, especially the *Vaishnavâite* tradition. He had striven all his life to become a beautiful soul worthy of divine *anugraha* or grace. He had eliminated all "impurities" and become as perfect as it was within his power to become. He had even surrendered his male identity and the last residual source of violence. He could go no further and had to await divine grace. If God thought him a fit vehicle, he would do His work through him. Otherwise, he stood helpless. That might perhaps explain why, having himself earlier described his experiments as *prayog*, he now called them *yajna*. Unlike a *prayog*, a *yajna* signified total self-surrender, a plaintive prayer and a desperate cry for help . . .

It would seem that most of Gandhi's critics were persuaded by his arguments. They restored their relations with him and said, both privately and in public, that they had done him a grave injustice.

Influenced by the works of Ruskin and Tolstoy, as well as the Bhagavadgita, Gandhi had become committed to the concept of bread labour. Gandhi took comfort in the thought that even the Bible said about the same thing: "With the sweat of thy brow thou shalt earn thy bread." Thus, Gandhi said, "Bodily labour is our lot in life; it is best then, to do it in the spirit of service and dedicate it to Shri Krishna. Anyone who works in that spirit all his life becomes free from evil and is delivered from all bonds."

Gandhi believed that bodily work would keep the devotee humble, whereas mental work might encourage tendencies towards the development of an *asuri* or proudly demonic intelligence. He felt that it was wrong to cultivate book-knowledge at the cost of body labour. Gandhi, besides, entertained another idea: that the best and simplest means to self-realisation or to being with God, was to serve God's creatures. He reasoned that God was incorporeal and not in need whereas fellow human beings were certainly corporeal and therefore in need. So what better way could there be to realise God than by way of service to humanity?

But who were the ones in need? Within the framework of service as faith, as the Jesuit priest Rev. Jesudasan was quick to note in his book on Gandhi, the Mahatma emphasised service to certain categories of persons. Gandhi had said, "The best and most understandable place where He can be worshipped is a living creature. The service of the distressed, the crippled and the helpless among living things constitutes worship of God." When, during the earthquake in Quetta in Baluchistan, several hundreds were killed, he wrote that such visitations should "humble us and prepare us to face our Maker whenever the call comes" and "teach us to be ever ready to share the sufferings of our fellows whoever they may be".

It is interesting that the law, that to live man must work, first came home to Gandhi upon reading Tolstoy's writing on bread labour. But even before that Gandhi had begun to pay homage to the law of labour after reading Ruskin's *Unto This Last*. The divine law, that man must earn his bread by labouring with his own hands was first stressed by a Russian writer named T. M. Bondaref. Tolstoy advertised it and gave it wide publicity. Commenting on this Gandhi wrote: "In my view the same principle has been set forth in the third chapter of the *Gita* where we are told that he who eats without offering sacrifice eats stolen food." Sacrifice in this context, Gandhi held, could only mean bread labour. He must have been referring to these lines from the Gita:

Ishtaanbhogaanhi vo devaa daasyante yajnabhaavitaahaa
Tairdattaanapradayaibhyo yo bhunkte stena eva sah
(Ch. III, *Shloka* 12)

(Propitiated by sacrifices, the gods will bestow on you the enjoyments you desire. He who enjoys these gifts bestowed by them without reciprocatory offering by way of repaying them is certainly a thief.)

Gandhi, surely, must also have been referring to another point made by Lord Krishna in the Gita when he said:

Yajnashishtaashinah santo muchyante sarvakilbishaih
Bhunjate te tvagham paapaa ye pachantyaatmakaaranaat
(Ch. III, *Shloka* 13)

(The righteous who partake the remains of the sacrifice are freed from all sins, but the impious who cook food just for their own selfish use, eat sin.)

Gandhi's logic was simple enough. He asked, "How can a man who does not do body labour have the right to eat? If everyone, whether rich or poor, has thus to take exercise in some form or shape, why should it not assume the form of productive, i.e. bread labour?" So, concluded Gandhi,

"Intelligent bread labour is any day the highest form of social service."

He explained why he used the word "intelligent" to describe bread labour. He noted that labour, to be social service, must have definite purpose behind it otherwise every labourer could be said to render social service. To Gandhi, social service meant something more, it meant labouring for the benefit and service of society. Gandhi further argued that obedience to the law of bread labour would bring about a silent revolution in the structure of society. Men's triumph would consist in substituting the struggle for existence by the struggle for mutual service. The law of the brute would be replaced by the law of man.

Gandhi was totally devoted to work. To him, work was worship. As he often repeated himself, there never could be too much emphasis placed on work. True service to man was impossible without bread labour, otherwise described in the Gita as *yajna*. It was only when a man or woman had done bodily labour for the sake of service that he or she had the right to live.

So particular was Gandhi about the importance of bread labour that he once said, "If I had the good fortune to be face to face with one like the Buddha, I should not hesitate to ask him why he did not teach the gospel of work in preference to one of contemplation. I should do the same thing if I were to meet . . . these saints [like Sant Tukaram and Jnanadev]."

It was not, as he explained, that he was against intellectual labour, which was important and had an undoubted place in the scheme of life. But what he insisted on was the necessity of physical labour. No man, claimed Gandhi, ought to be free from that obligation which would serve to improve even the quality of his intellectual output.

To Gandhi, work was related to *yajna* or sacrifice. *Yajna*, however, had a deeper meaning. It meant an act performed without attachment, directed to the welfare of others, done without desiring any return for it, whether of a temporal or spiritual nature. In the Gita it is said:

Karmanyevaadhikaaraste maa phaleshu kadaachana
   (Ch. II, *Shloka* 47)

(On action alone be thy interest, never on its fruits.)

He defined *yajna* thus: "It [*yajna*] is duty to be performed, or service to be rendered, all the twenty four hours of the day ... To serve without desire is to favour not others, but ourselves, even as in discharging a debt we serve only ourselves, lighten our burden and fulfil our duty. Again, not only the good, but all of us are bound to place our resources at the disposal of humanity. And if such is the law, as evidently it is, indulgence ceases to hold a place in life and gives way to renunciation. The duty of renunciation differentiates mankind from the beast."

Yajna, Gandhi held, is a life of sacrifice and is the pinnacle of art and is full of joy. *Yajna* meant giving up one's weaknesses and passions, and sacrificing one's all for the good of humanity. *Yajna* was not *yajna* if one felt it to be burdensome or annoying, and therefore, an essential feature of *yajna* was serving others. Self-indulgence led to destruction, and renunciation to immortality. Joy had no independent existence. It depended upon our attitude to life. And to that, he added:

> One who would serve will not waste a thought upon his own comforts, which he leaves to be attended to or neglected by his Master on high. He will not, therefore, encumber himself with everything that comes his way; he will take only what he strictly needs and leave the rest. He will be calm, free from anger and unruffled in mind even if he finds himself inconvenienced. His service, like virtue, is its own reward, and he will rest content with it.

What he aimed for was to be a *sthitaprajna*, one who lives in total equanimity. And what, according to Gandhi, were the characteristics of a *sthitaprajna*?

> He is one who withdraws his senses from the objects of the senses behind the shield of the spirit, as a tortoise does its limbs under its shell. A man whose wisdom is not steady is liable to be betrayed into anger, evil thoughts or abuse. On the contrary, the man with steady wisdom will remain equally unaffected by adulation or abuse. He will realise that abuse fouls only the tongue that utters it, never the person against whom it is hurled. A man of steady wisdom will, therefore, never wish ill to anyone, but will pray even for his enemy with his last breath.

Rev. Jesudasan has analysed Gandhi's thoughts even more beautifully. He says, "Gandhi identified as hypothetical the conflict between love for God and love for humanity; such seeming disparity was, in fact, a conflict within a person, requiring an inner search and then purification. The idea of a divorce between the two loves was predicated on the base motives of self-love and self-gratification." Real love for humanity was impossible without love for God, Gandhi strongly believed.

Gandhi was a firm believer in the concept that the heart's earnest and *pure* desire is always fulfilled. As he stated, "For me the road to salvation lies through incessant toil in the service of my country and there through of humanity. I want to identify myself with everything that lives."

Gandhi further said that he had no desire for the perishable kingdom of earth. His desire was for striving for the Kingdom of Heaven, which is moksha. To attain that end it was not necessary for him to seek the shelter of a cave. "I carry one about me, if I would but know it," he added. The God he sought was within him, if only he could find him. That, incidentally, is what Kabir said in his *doha*:

> *Jaise til mein tel hai,*
> *Jyon chakmak mein aag,*
> *Tera sayeen tujh mein hai,*
> *Tu jaag sake toh jaag.*

(Like seed contains oil, and flint stone fire, your Lord is within you, realise Him if you can.)

So Gandhi strove to find his God everywhere and in everything. He did not find him as he would have wished. But as he claimed, he knew the path and he rejoiced to walk on it. He wept when he slipped. But he remembered the words: *He who strove never perished.* To him striving was all. Striving and faith. As he admitted: "I am a man of faith. My reliance is solely on God. One step is enough for me. The next step He will make clear to me when the time for it comes." So defeat never disheartened him. How could it for one who had complete faith in God? He wrote: "It can only chasten me . . . I know that God will guide me. Truth is superior to man's wisdom. I have never lost my optimism. In seemingly darkest hours, hope has burnt bright within me. I cannot kill the hope myself. I must say I cannot give an ocular demonstration to justify the hope. But there is no defeat in me."

He trusted people and often felt let down. Many deceived him but he never repented his association with them. His theory was that "the most practical, the most dignified way of going on in the world is to take people at their word when you have no positive reason to the contrary". On this issue his philosophy was simple. He wrote: "I believe in trusting. Trust begets trust. Suspicion is foetid and only stinks. He who trusts has never yet lost in the world."

Gandhi often spoke about his "inner voice". Cynics questioned this inner voice that he articulated at critical times in his life. Gandhi explained it thus:

> There come to us moments in life when about some things we need no proof from without. A little voice within tells us: "You are on the right track, move neither to your left nor right, but keep to the straight and narrow way."

Emphasising the importance of the inner voice he also added:

> There are moments in your life when you must act, even though you cannot carry your best friends with you. The "still small voice" within you must always be the final arbiter when there is a conflict of duty.

Some charitable critics would describe Gandhi's dependence on his inner voice as just hallucination. Gandhi had no quarrel with them at all. He stated in plain words: "You have to believe no one but yourselves. You must try to listen to the inner voice but if you will not have the expression 'inner voice' you may use the expression 'dictates of reason' which you should obey and if you will not parade God, I have no doubt you will parade something else which in the end will prove to be God, for, fortunately, there is no one and nothing else but God in this universe."

For Gandhi, his inner voice was God, none else. As he wrote:

> For me the Voice of God, of Conscience, of Truth or the Inner Voice or "the still small voice" mean one and the same thing. I saw no form. I have never tried, for I have always believed God to be without form. But what I did hear was like a Voice from afar and yet quite near. It was as unmistakable as

some human voice definitely speaking to me, and irresistible. I was not dreaming at the time I heard the Voice. The hearing of the Voice was preceded by a terrific struggle within me. Suddenly the Voice came upon me. I listened, made certain that it was the Voice, and the struggle ceased. I was calm. The determination was made accordingly, the date and the hour of the fast were fixed."

He did not go out of his way to convince the sceptic. He honestly admitted that he had no evidence to prove that what he heard was his inner voice and it was not merely his imagination. The sceptic was welcome to conclude that he was deluding himself, said Gandhi, but he was convinced that whatever the opinion of the world, it would not deter him from the conviction that he had heard the voice of God.

In this regard Gandhi permitted no argument. His mind was absolutely clear and if anyone thought that God was a creation of one's own imagination, he had no quarrel with that view either. Making this clear he wrote:

If that view holds good, then nothing is real, everything is of our imagination. Even so, whilst my imagination dominates me, I can only act under its spell. Realest things are only relatively so. For me the Voice was more real than my own existence. It has never failed me, and for that matter, anyone else.

And everyone who wills can hear the Voice. It is within everyone. But like everything else, it requires previous and definite preparation.

What was this "preparation" that Gandhi referred to? It meant training, an intense training to learn to differentiate between what was God's Voice and what could be the Devil's. Once, dealing with the objection raised by the scientists, Gandhi said:

When a man speaks of the "inner voice", the scientist says it is auto-suggestion. It is auto-suggestion indeed, because God is within. When he says it is auto-suggestion, to him it appears a thing to be despised and suppressed. I, however, use the word "auto-suggestion" in my own sense... When the scientist speaks of the inner voice being auto-suggestion, he means to say it is the devil's voice. Maybe it is. There are occasions when the devil's voice speaks as God's Voice. God's Voice is not heard in the heart of every person. It is no matter of inherent right. You must undergo a course of training, if you want to hear the Voice of God. There are some rules laid down for it. If you follow them, the result would be infallible.

It is interesting that even someone like Jawaharlal Nehru, who was by no means religiously inclined, and at best can be described as an agnostic, could take Gandhi's inner voice as acceptable. In his *An Autobiography* Nehru has this to say:

I knew that Gandhiji usually acts on instinct (I prefer to call it that than the "inner voice" or an answer to prayer) and very often that instinct is right. He has repeatedly shown what a wonderful knack he has of sensing the mass mind and of acting at the psychological moment. The reasons, which afterwards adduce to justify his action are usually afterthoughts and seldom carry one very far. A leader or a man of action in a crisis almost always acts subconsciously and then thinks of the reasons for his action. I felt also that Gandhiji had acted rightly in suspending civil resistance. But the reason he had given seemed to me an insult to intelligence and an amazing performance for a leader of a national movement.

That is the intellectual and sceptical Nehru speaking. Dr. Sarvapalli Radhakrishnan, the philosopher had his own interpretation of what Gandhi called his "inner voice". Radhakrishnan distinguished between the "immediacy which appears at the sub-intellectual level (feeling) and the immediacy which appeared at the supra-intellectual level (intuition), the latter of which he regarded as "to some extent the result of discursive thinking". And then Radhakrishnan went on to say:

> Plato and Sankara agree that this kind of intuitive certainty is reached after a long process of discursive analysis. When once the intuition is reached, it is prolonged into an intellectual ordering of images and concepts. All dynamic acts of thinking, whether in a game of chess or a mathematical problem are controlled by an intuitive grasp of the situation as a whole . . . There is no break of continuity between intuition and intellect. In moving from intellect to intuition, we are not moving in the direction of unreason, but we are getting into the deepest rationality of which human nature is capable. In it we think more profoundly, feel more deeply and see more truly. We see, feel and become in obedience to our whole nature, and not simply measure things by the fragmentary standard of conduct. We think with a certain totality or wholeness . . . Intuition is not independent of intellect; it is the crown of the intellectual process.

It is not for ordinary mortals to sit in judgement on Gandhiji's claims to the soundness of his inner voice. If it is mere instinct, as Nehru asserts, what Gandhi did under its influence often turned out to be right. Chandrashanker Shukla, in his *Gandhi's View of Life*, cites five instances when Gandhi acted according to what his inner voice told him to do, as in his decision not to go to Europe in 1926, the suspension of civil disobedience for six weeks in May 1933, the addition of village industries to *khadi* in January 1934, his reaction to the communal award in 1934, and finally his decision to retire from the 4-*anna* membership of the Congress. Henry Brailsford, an objective critic of Gandhi comments: "Gandhiji did not plan it so, but in fact, the series of five struggles he led, wave after wave, with intervals for recovery in India and reflection in England, was the best strategy that he could have followed." Gandhi gave credit for his decisions to his inner voice. Others, more cynical, gave it to his sound intuition.

To Gandhi, work was worship, and worship was a way to God. It naturally followed that the *charkha* or the spinning wheel was a way to reach God through physical labour. Indeed, he was to say, "I have described my spinning as a penance or sacrament. And, since I believe that where there is pure and active love for the poor, there is God also, I see God in every thread that I draw on the spinning wheel."

His advice to congressmen, indeed to all Indians, was that they should take to spinning. He told his readers, "The music of the wheel will be as balm to your soul. I believe that the yarn we spin is capable of mending the broken warp and woof of our life. The *charkha* is the symbol of non-violence on which all life, if it is to be real life, must be based."

Once Gandhi set up his ashram, spinning became a part and parcel of the ashram prayer. Gandhi linked the concept of spinning as sacrifice, with the idea of God, on the grounds that the *charkha* offered hope of salvation to the poor. He said, "I do not know whether I am a Karmayogi or any other Yogi. I know that I cannot live without work. I crave to die with my hand at the spinning wheel. If one has to establish communion with God through some means, why not through the spinning wheel? 'Him who worships Me,' says the Lord in the *Gita*, 'I guide along the right path and see to his needs.'"

The *charkha* movement in India came into existence in 1920, as Gandhi, during his travels across the country began to notice the utter poverty in which the people lived in villages. How were they to be delivered from a life of total deprivation? If service to man was service to God, serving the peasant, whom Gandhi described as *daridranarayan,* was worshipping God. The *charkha* was not a new discovery. It was not a new invention, insofar as Indian peasantry was concerned. As Charles Andrews described it: "It is a re-discovery, like the discovery of its own mother by a strayed child." The poor peasant needed some sustenance. He could not depend on government or a maharaja for his daily meal. The cotton industry in urban areas could not sustain the village unemployed. After seventy years of cotton industry, and having some fifty crores of capital, the cotton magnates in the early twenties of the twentieth century could not provide bread to more than 1.5 million souls, representing the families of some 3,70,000 mill-hands employed by them. So where were the rest of the unemployed to go? It was then that Gandhi thought up the *charkha* as a means of earning one's daily bowl of rice. He never put forward spinning on the *charkha* as a principal occupation. It was offered to those who would otherwise be starving. Spinning on the *charkha* was immediately practicable because it did not require any capital or costly implements to become operative. Using the *charkha* did not need any high degree of skill or intelligence and could be achieved through very little exertion. Another advantage of the spinning wheel was that it was not dependent on the erratic Indian monsoon and a person could spin any time of the day or night. The *charkha* alone could effectively solve the problem of unemployment, as it carried work to the very cottage of the peasant, who, consequently, did not have to be submissive to any landlord or money lender. Spinning on the *charkha* gave the unemployed, starving peasant back his self-respect. Gandhi not only realised it, but made it part of his fight for independence. For Gandhi, spinning was not an alternative to work in an industry. As he succinctly worded it: "Hand-spinning does not, it is not intended that it should, compete with, in order to displace, any existing type of industry; it does not aim at withdrawing a single able-bodied person who can otherwise find a remunerative occupation from his work. The sole claim advanced on its behalf is that it alone offers an immediate, practicable and permanent solution of that problem of problems that confronts India, viz. the enforced idleness of nearly six months in the year of an overwhelming majority of India's population, owing to lack of a suitable supplementary occupation to agriculture and the chronic starvation of the masses that results therefrom."

And he was to add: "I have not contemplated, much less advised, the abandonment of a single healthy, life-giving industrial activity for the sake of hand-spinning. The entire foundation of the spinning wheel rests on the fact that there are crores of semi-employed people in India. And I should admit that if there were none such, there would be no room for the spinning wheel."

Through the spinning wheel Gandhi hoped to bring succour to the starving and the unemployed in the country. If a village perishes, Gandhi would say, it would be India that would perish, with the result that its own mission in the world would be lost. The spinning wheel, in the circumstances, was Gandhi's way of worshipping God.

It was Gandhi's claim that God appeared to him in myriad forms. And one of the forms was the *charkha*. Encouraging the poor to use the *charkha* was a direct means to serving God. He held that "he who spins before the poor inviting them to do likewise serves God as no one else does". Addressing a public meeting at Kanaddukathan where he was presented a purse by some of the rich merchants and money-lenders, Gandhi said: "The greatest charity at the present moment that I can conceive for any Indian to do is undoubtedly to promote *Khadi* work." And later he wrote: "To those who are hungry and unemployed God can dare reveal Himself only as work and wages as the assurance of food." And to the women in his ashram he wrote: "Please remember that all of you are tied to Mother India with a cord of hand-spun yarn. If you give up spinning, you give up service too. Do not, therefore, neglect the spinning wheel. Today Rama dwells in the spinning wheel. God always reveals Himself to us in some concrete shape. That is why we sing of Draupadi, that for her, God took the form of garments. Anyone who desires to see God today may see Him in the form of the spinning wheel."

To one of his disciples, Krishnachandra, he said, "While plying the *takli*, fix your mind on the thought that it is God who is doing it, that He is in every fibre of the yarn. See Him with the inner eye. Then spinning, which now seems secondary to you, will become the primary thing. In the language of satyagraha, the means become identified with the end."

As Gandhi saw it, using the *charkha* was a way of communing with God. He believed that *swadeshi* was the power that would take us towards God and that spinning was a way of imitating God's own active action.

In a way, spinning, to Gandhi, became an obsession. As he wrote in *Young India*, the revival of hand-spinning and hand-weaving would not make the largest contribution to the economic and moral regeneration of India. But being a practical man he saw that the millions must have a simple industry to supplement agriculture. Spinning had been the cottage industry in India for decades past and if millions of people had to be saved from starvation, Gandhi felt that they must be enabled to re-introduce spinning in their homes. Writing with a passion that only he was capable of, Gandhi insisted that spinning was the fittest and most acceptable sacrificial labour. He felt there was nothing nobler than doing the labour that the poor do, for at least an hour a day. This was a means of identifying with the poor, and through them with mankind, thus serving God.

Writing as late as April 1940 he was pushing the *charkha* with single-minded devotion. He wrote:

> The revival [of *charkha*] cannot take place without an army of selfless Indians of intelligence and patriotism working with a single mind in the villages to spread the message of the *charkha* and bring a ray of hope and light into their lustreless eyes. This is a mighty effort at co-operation and adult education of the correct type. It brings about a silent and sure revolution like the silent but sure and life-giving revolution of the *charkha*.

Gandhi truly believed that if he could make the spinning wheel the foundation on which a sound village life could be built, and the industry of *khadi* was revived, all other industries would follow. He argued that the *charkha* was "the symbol of non-violent economic self-sufficiency". Once villagers took to the *charkha*, there would be no need to look for alms from the rich. And on yet another occasion he wrote with equal passion:"We shall without effort become the centre of hope and the people will come to us of their own accord. Every village will become the nerve-centre of independent India. India will then not be known by her cities like Bombay and Calcutta, but by her 400 million inhabiting the seven lakhs of villages. The problem of Hindu-Muslim differences, untouchability, conflicts, misunderstandings and rivalries will all melt away."

Gandhi was convinced that India's economy would be strengthened and enriched by the hand-spun cloth produced in her villages. Khadi, he felt, could raise the village to unknown heights and was "the sun of the village solar system". According to him the spinning wheel was a symbol not of commercial war but of commercial peace. It bore not a message of ill-will towards the nations of the earth but of goodwill and self-help. It would not need the protection of a navy threatening a world's peace and exploiting its resources but the *religious* determination of millions to spin their yarn in their own homes just as they cook their food in their own homes. In a sense, spinning, to Gandhi, was almost tantamount to a religious duty.

The protection of every form of life on earth was a natural corollary to Gandhi's staunch belief in ahimsa. This defence of all creation manifested itself in the form of cow protection. He once wrote: "Hinduism believes in the oneness not merely of all human life, but in the oneness of all that lives. Its worship of the cow is, in my opinion, its unique contribution to the evolution of humanitarianism. It is a practical application of the belief in the oneness and, therefore, sacredness of all life. The great belief in transmigration is a direct consequence of that belief."

Gandhi described the cow as "a poem on pity". As he saw it, protection of the cow, the "purest type of sub-human life", meant protection of the whole dumb creation of God. So deeply conscious he was of the cow, which he called the "purest type of sub-human life", that he even went to the extent of saying that he worshipped it and "shall defend its worship against the whole world". To quote him further:

> Mother cow is in many ways better than the mother who gave us birth. Our mother gives us milk for a couple of years and then expects us to serve her when we grow up. Mother cow expects from us nothing but grass and grain. Our mother often falls ill and expects service from us. Mother cow rarely falls ill. Here is an unbroken record of service which does not end with her death.

Gandhi considered that "the central fact of Hinduism is cow protection", that cow protection "is the gift of Hinduism to the world" and that "Hinduism will live so long as there are Hindus to protect the cow". He went even further. He said, "Hindus will be judged not by their *tilaks*, not by the correct chanting of *mantras*, not by their pilgrimages, not by their most punctilious observances of caste rules, but their ability to protect the cow."

Gandhi said that cow protection to him was not mere protection of the cow but the protection of all animate and powerless creatures in the world. To him, in the finer spiritual sense, cow protection meant the practice of ahimsa as a way of reaching God. Gandhi acknowledged that one did not attain moksha by mere practice of cow protection. To truly attain moksha one had to combine various other means too and purify oneself of negative emotions like anger, jealousy, and hatred. "It follows, therefore," Gandhi said, "that the meaning of cow protection in terms of *Moksha* must be much wider and far more comprehensive than is commonly supposed. The cow protection which can bring one *Moksha* must, from its very nature, include the protection of everything that feels. Therefore in my opinion, every little breach of the Ahimsa principle, like causing hurt by harsh speech to anyone, man, woman or child, to cause pain to the weakest and the most insignificant creature on earth would be a breach of the principle of cow protection, would be tantamount to the sin of beef-eating—differing from it in degree if at all, rather than in kind." In view of this definition, Gandhi rued the fact that we could not claim to be following the principle of cow protection.

Gandhi firmly believed that Hinduism was deeply rooted in ahimsa. It was this belief in the right of all living beings to freedom from violence that had made Gandhi feel revulsion and horror on witnessing the sacrifice of goats to Kali. It was this same conviction in the dignity of life that made him oppose untouchability for "a religion that establishes the worship of the cow cannot possibly countenance or warrant a cruel and inhuman boycott of human beings".

In the circumstances, fighting untouchability also became part of Gandhi's search for God. So strongly was he against untouchability that he said that if untouchability lives, Hinduism must die and that he would far rather that Hindusim died than that untouchability lived. He did not believe in caste. As he saw it, caste had nothing to do with religion. It was a custom of whose origin he had not the faintest idea, but knowing or not knowing its origin had nothing to do with his spiritual hunger. At a discourse he gave at the Gandhi Seva Sangh in 1937, he said, "My God is myriad-formed, and while sometimes I see Him in the spinning wheel, at other times I see Him in communal unity, then again in removal of untouchability; and that is how I establish communion with Him according as the Spirit moves me."

His understanding of God and untouchability sometimes went to unacceptable lengths. When there was a terrible earthquake in Bihar, Gandhi made a statement that even elicited a strong censure from Rabindranath Tagore. Gandhi said, "Visitations like droughts, floods, earthquakes and the like, though they seem to have only physical origins, are, for me, somehow connected with man's morals. Therefore, I instinctively felt that the earthquake was a visitation for the sin of untouchability . . . My belief is a call to repentance and self-purification." In a speech he delivered in Mysore in 1927, he was just as immoveable in this regard: "Lord Krishna has taught that to be a true *bhakta* we should make no difference between a Brahmin and a scavenger. If that is true there can be no place for untouchability in Hinduism."

His logic was impeccable. C. F. Andrews remembers what Gandhi once said about Rama who was rowed across the Ganga by one regarded as an "untouchable". If Rama could accept the services of a supposed untouchable, Gandhi argued, how can anyone possibly conceive the idea of any human being dismissed as an "untouchable"? So, said Gandhi, "The fact that we addressed God as 'the purifier of the polluted' shows that it is a sin to regard anyone being born in Hinduism as polluted. I have hence been never tired of repeating that it is a great sin." A Harijan leader wrote to Gandhiji wondering how one could serve God when "we do not know God". Gandhi's reply was instantaneous. He said, "We may not know God, but we know His creation. Service of His creation is the service of God."

Gandhi wanted untouchability to be completely erased from Hindu society. It did not worry him that in this he may fail. He said, "In battling against untouchability and in dedicating myself to that battle, I have no less an ambition than to see a complete regeneration of humanity. It may be a mere dream, as unreal as the silver in the sea-shell. It is not so to me while the dream lasts and in the words of Romain Rolland: 'Victory lies not in realization of the goal but in a relentless pursuit of it.'" Relentless he was. In 1935, he undertook a journey throughout the length and breadth of the country and in some places, like Pune, invited the wrath of Brahmins who stoned his car. It was known as his Harijan tour. He may not have won many people to his point of view but he made his point alright.

What needs to be remembered is that for Gandhi every act in life, every passing phenomenon, was part of living and to live was to look for God. His Hinduism was not sectarian. It included all that he knew was best in all religions whether it was Islam, Christianity, Buddhism, or Zoroastrianism. He claimed that he approached politics too as he did everything else, in a religious spirit.

In one of his many articles on the subject Gandhi averred that he could not be leading a religious life unless he identified himself with the whole of mankind and that he could not do so unless he took part in politics. As he saw it, the whole gamut of man's activities constituted an indivisible whole. He wrote: "You cannot divide social, economic, political and purely religious work into watertight compartments. I do not know any religion apart from human activity. It provides a moral basis to all other activities which they would otherwise lack, reducing life to a maze of 'sound and fury, signifying nothing'."

For Gandhi, politics bereft of religion was "absolute dirt, ever to be shunned". Strong words, but where matters concerning spirituality were involved, Gandhi was not going to turn soft. In such instances he would not compromise. He possibly could not, being Gandhi. As he pointed out, politics concerned nations and that which concerned the welfare of nations should necessarily be one of the concerns of a man who was religiously inclined, "in other words, a seeker after God and Truth". In the same vein he wrote: "For me, God and Truth are convertible terms and if anyone told me God was a God of untruth or a God of torture, I would decline to worship him. Therefore, in politics also, we have to establish the Kingdom of Heaven."

It is remarkable that Gandhi associated God even with politics. For Gandhi, God, as always, was the master of the play, in whose hands he was merely a plaything. And he never hid his thoughts. Thus, in a letter to Durga Desai in January 1931 he explained why he had declined to attend a round Table Conference held in London to discuss problems related to India's struggle for freedom. He wrote: "My heart simply did not consent, however much I tried to persuade myself. The reins are held by that Master of the Play. Why, then, need we worry at all? On the contrary, we should daily leave the reins more and more in His hands and strengthen His hands."

And then there was that other great occasion when he accepted an invitation to participate in discussions that were to lead to what came to be known as the Gandhi-Irwin pact. Of that he wrote to Prabhashankar Pattani in February 1931:

> I always pray to God that I, who am standing at death's door, may not put my signature to anything which might prove a trap for the country. I am going to Delhi today with this prayer in my heart. I do not feel presumptuous like the dog in the story who was walking under the cart. I know the limits of my strength. I am but a particle of dust. Even such a particle has a place in God's creation, provided it submits to being trodden on. Everything is done by that Supreme Potter. He may use me as He wills.

Throughout his life, Gandhi saw himself, in every activity he undertook, merely as a servant of God and thus a servant of humanity. The report of the thirty-ninth Indian National Congress (1924) quotes him as tracing the value of his life to this calling: "My time is valuable, for I deem myself a servant of God."

When, in 1933, he went on a fast for the Harijan cause, Gandhi answered the critical appeals of General Smuts, C. Rajagopalachari, Dr. M. S. Ansari, and his own son Devdas, along the same lines:

> My claim to hear the voice of God is no new claim. Unfortunately there is no way that I know of proving the claim except through results. God will not be God if He allowed Himself to be object of proof by His creatures. But he does give His willing slave the power to pass through the fiercest

of ordeals. I have been a willing slave to this most exacting Master for more than half a century. His voice has been increasingly audible as the years have rolled by.

Gandhi was agreeable to attend the second Round Table Conference—he had declined to attend the first—held in London as the sole representative of the Congress. How come? Gandhi provided the answer:

> I must go to London with God as my only guide. He is a jealous Lord. He will allow no one to share His authority. One has therefore to appear before Him in all one's weakness, empty-handed and in a spirit of full surrender, and then He enables you to stand before a whole world and protects you from harm.

"God," claimed Gandhi, "is always at the service of his devotees, he is ever the Servant of his Servants and he justifies the devotee's faith." It was his belief that there was a mysterious, power that pervaded everything though one could not see it.

Gandhi held that God is in the heart of man, that prayer does for the purification of the mind what the bucket and broom do for the cleaning up of our physical surrounding, and that a temple is where God is.

As always what mattered most to Gandhi was prayer—and faith. As he put it, "I do have a living faith in a living God. A living, immoveable faith is all that is required for reaching the full spiritual height attainable by human beings. God is not outside this earthly case of ours ... We can feel Him if we will but withdraw ourselves from the senses. The Divine Music is incessantly going on within ourselves, but the loud senses drown the delicate music which is unlike, and infinitely superior to, anything that we can perceive or hear with our senses."

Once a missionary Dr. Mott, asked Gandhi what had brought deepest satisfaction to his soul in difficulties and doubts and questionings. Gandhi's answer was simple—and to the point. He said, "Living faith in God."

Dr. Mott continued, "When have you had indubitable manifestation of God in your life and experience?"

Gandhi quietly replied, "I have seen and believed that God never appears to you in person, but in action which can only account for your deliverance in your darkest hour."

Somewhat puzzled, Dr. Mott asked, "You mean, things take place that cannot possibly happen apart from God?"

To that question Gandhi gave a detailed answer. He recounted an event that took place in the thirties when he went on a twenty-one day fast for the removal of untouchability. In words that still reverberate in many hearts, he said, "Yes. They happen suddenly and unawares. One experience stands quite distinctly in my memory. It relates to my twenty-one day fast for the removal of untouchability. I had gone to sleep the night before without the slightest idea of having to declare a fast the next morning. At about 12 o'clock in the night something wakes me suddenly, and some Voice—within or without—I cannot say, whispers: 'Thou must go on a fast.'

'How many days?' I ask.

The Voice again says: 'Twenty-one days.'

'When does it begin?' I ask.

It says: 'You begin tomorrow.'

"I went quietly off to sleep after making the decision. I did not tell anything to my companions until after the morning prayer. I placed into their hands a slip of paper announcing my decision and asking them not to argue with me as the decision was irrevocable.

"Well, the doctors thought that I would not survive the fast. But something within me said that I would, and that I must go forward. That kind of experience has never in my life happened before or after that date."

To Gandhi, then, God meant everything. He acted according to the will of God. As he said in so many words, "I could not live for a single second without religion. Many of my political friends despair of me because they say that even my politics are derived from religion. And they are right. My politics and all other activities of mine are derived from my religion. I go further and say that every activity of a man of religion must be derived from his religion, because religion means being bound to God, that is to say God rules your every breath."

More, he wrote: "It is faith that steers us through stormy seas, faith that moves mountains and faith that jumps across the ocean. That faith is nothing but a living, wide-awake consciousness of God within. He who has achieved that faith wants nothing. Bodily diseased, he is spiritually healthy; physically poor, he rolls in spiritual riches."

Reflecting an aspect of Hinduism in which God was seen in many forms, Gandhi said, "The forms are many, but the informing spirit is one. How can there be room for distinctions of high and low where there is this all-embracing, fundamental unity underlying the outward diversity? For that is a fact meeting you at every step in daily life. The final goal of all religions is to realise this essential oneness."

In another one of his articles Gandhi reminded his readers that in his early youth he was taught to repeat what, in Hindu scriptures, are known as the one thousand names of God. But, Gandhi pointed out, those one thousand names of God were by no means exhaustive. "We believe," he noted, "and I think it is the truth, that God has as many names as there are creatures. Therefore, we also say that God is nameless, and since God has many forms, we consider him formless and since He speaks through many tongues we consider him to be speechless and so on." And he added, "When I came to study Islam, I found Islam too had many names of God."

In his long and continuous, not to say relentless, search for God, Gandhi first had come to the conclusion that God is Truth, but then it finally dawned on him that it is not that God is Truth, but that Truth is God. It took him, on his own submission, about fifty years to arrive at that final understanding of God. He then found that the nearest approach to truth was through love. It sounded beautiful but then Gandhi also realised that "love" has many meanings in the English language and that human love in the sense of passion could become a degrading thing. Discussing this dilemma, Gandhi wrote: "I found, too, that love in the sense of ahimsa had only a limited number of votaries in the world. But I never found a double meaning in connection with truth and even atheists had not demurred to the necessity of power of truth."

Atheists, wrote Gandhi, in their passion for discovering truth, did not hesitate to deny the very existence of God. It was because of that reasoning that he decided that instead of saying God is Truth, he should say Truth is God. In his decision to change his definition, Gandhi says he also had to take into consideration the fact that millions had taken the name of God and committed nameless atrocities in His name. That fact had to be noted. In Sanskrit the word for truth is *sat*—a word which literally means "that which exists". God alone *is* and nothing else exists and the same truth was emphasised and exemplified in the *Kalma* of Islam. Hence, Gandhi said, for these and many other reasons he came to the conclusion that the definition—Truth is God—gave him the greatest satisfaction. And to that he added, "When you want to find Truth as God, the only inevitable means is love, that is, non-violence and since I believe that ultimately the means and ends are convertible terms, I should not hesitate to say that God is Love."

As Gandhi saw it, from the standpoint of pure truth, the body too was a possession and it was a desire for enjoyment that created bodies for the soul. When that desire vanished there remained no further need for the body and man was freed from the vicious circle of births and deaths. Wrote Gandhi: "The soul is omnipresent; why should she care to be confined within the cage-like body or do evil and even kill for the sake of that cage? We thus arrive at the ideal of total renunciation and learn to use the body for the purposes of service so long as it exists, so much so that service, and not bread, becomes with us the staff of life. We eat and drink, sleep and wake, for service alone. Such an attitude of mind brings us real happiness and the beatific vision in the fullness of time."

Gandhi called himself a *sanatanist* Hindu, one of the reasons being that he did not disbelieve in idol worship. He understood why people worshipped idols. But he said, "A book, a building, a picture, a carving are surely all images in which God does reside, but they are not God. He who says that, errs." Writing in *Harijan* (1940) he explained this further. He wrote:

> Idolatry is bad, not so idol-worship. An idolator makes a fetish of his idol. An idol-worshipper sees God even in a stone and therefore takes the help of an idol to establish his union with God. Every Hindu child knows that the stone in the famous temple in Banaras is not Kashi Vishwanath. But he believes that the Lord of the Universe does reside specially in that stone. This play of the imagination is permissible and healthy.

But if he did not particularly favour idols he fully saw the necessity of temples. And this, too, he explained in his writings in *Harijan*:

> I know of no religion or sect that has done or is doing without its House of God, variously described as a temple, mosque, church, synagogue or *agiari*. Nor is it certain that any of the great reformers including Jesus destroyed or discarded temples

altogether... I have ceased to visit temples for years, but I do not regard myself on that account as a better person than before ... There are millions whose faith is sustained through these temples, churches and mosques. They are not all blind followers of a superstition, nor are they fanatics ... To reject the necessity of temples is to reject the necessity of God, religion and earthly existence.

He called upon his readers to approach temples with faith. He said:

We, the human family, are not all philosophers. We are of the earth, very earthy and we are not satisfied with contemplating the Invisible God. Somehow or other, we want something which we can touch, something that we can see, something before which we can kneel down ... I ask you to approach temples not as if they represented a body of superstitions. If you approach these temples with faith in them, you will know each time you visit them that you will come away from them purified and with your faith more and more in the living God.

It depends on our mental condition whether we gain something or do not gain anything by going to the temples. We have to approach these temples in a humble and penitent mood ... And so, when we approach these temples, we must cleanse our bodies, our minds and our hearts and we should enter them in a prayerful mood and ask God to make us purer men and purer women for having entered their portals.

If Gandhi saw the necessity of temples, he also advocated temple reform. His continued struggle to gain entry into temples for Harijans ran parallel to his hope for radical change in the attitudes of priests as well as worshippers. As he rightly pointed out, if the inward spirit underwent change, the outward form would take care of itself.

Gandhi did not believe in idol worship and his only God was truth. But he was an ardent believer in invoking the name of Rama and reciting *Ramanama*. To him, reciting *Ramanama* was an end in itself. He referred to this frequently in his talks and in his writings. At a students' meeting in Rangoon, Burma, in April 1929, when someone asked him how to get rid of the Devil, he advised him to kneel before God and say *Ramanama*. As late as 1947, asserting that the straight way to cultivate *brahmacharya* was *Ramanama*, he wrote in *Harijan*: "I can say this from experience. Devotees and sages like Tulsidas have shown us this royal path." He said that it was his conviction that the orthodox aids to *brahmacharya* were of no significance compared to *Ramanama* when the Lord's name was enshrined in one's heart. And he went further to say, "The eleven rules of conduct are the means to enable us to reach God. Of the eleven rules Truth is the means and God called Rama is the end. Is it not equally true that Ramanama is the means and Truth is the end?" Gandhi admitted that he was a lover and devotee of Tulsidas. He admired him for offering the world a means to salvation through the mantra of *Ramanama*. To those who would listen to him, he would suggest that they join him in congregational prayer and chant *Ramanama*. In a long article written originally in Gujarati, Gandhi pointed out that a devotee of Rama "may be said to be the same as the steadfast one (*sthithaprajna*) of the *Gita*". Such a man, he said, will take God's name with every breath. "His Rama will be awake even whilst the body is asleep. Rama will always be with him in whatever he does." So totally committed was Gandhi to *Ramanama* that he once told a friend, "Ramanama to me is all-sufficing. There are as many names of God as His manifestations, but sages have, as a result of their life-long penance, devised names to be uttered by the devotees, in order to be able to commune with the Nameless. There are other *mantras* than Ramanama, but for me that is supreme . . . I may even say that the Word is in my heart, if not actually on my lips, all the twenty-four hours. It has been my saviour and I am ever stayed on it. In the spiritual literature of the world, the Ramayana of Tulasidas takes a foremost place."

But how was one to install *Ramanama* in the heart? In a reply he gave in *Harijan*, Gandhi conceded that it required "infinite patience". It might even take ages, but he said, the effort was worthwhile. Explaining still further, he said, "Ramanama could not come from the heart unless one had cultivated the virtues of truth, honesty and purity within and without." But even if there was no purity, the mere recitation of *Ramanama* was also a means for acquiring purity. He wrote: "I believe there is special merit in the recitation of Ramanama. If anyone knows that God is in truth residing in his heart, I admit that for him there is no need for recitation. But I have not known such a person. On the contrary, my personal experience tells me that there is something quite extraordinary in the recitation of Ramanama." It is difficult to imagine anyone in India who could be more passionate about *Ramanama* than Gandhi. A February 1946 issue of *Harijan* ran a question and answer article in which Gandhi sought to dispel doubts raised by one of his readers. It went thus:

QUESTIONER: While in conversation or doing brain work or when one is suddenly worried, can one recite Ramanama in one's heart? Do people do so at such times, and if so, how?

GANDHI: Experience shows that man can do so at any time, even in sleep, provided Ramanama is enshrined in his heart. If the taking of the name has become a habit, its recitation through the heart becomes as natural as the heart beat. Otherwise, Ramanama is a mere mechanical performance or at best has touched the heart only on the surface. When Ramanama has established its dominion over the heart, the question of vocal recitation does not arise. Because then it transcends speech. But it may well be held that persons who have attained this state are few and far between.

There is no doubt whatsoever that Ramanama contains all the power that is attributed to it. No one can, by mere wishing, enshrine Ramanama in his heart. Untiring effort is required as also patience. What an amount of labour and patience has been lavished by men to acquire the non-existent philosopher's stone? Surely, God's name is of infinitely richer value and always existent.

QUESTIONER: Is it harmful if, owing to stress or exigencies of work, one is unable to carry out daily devotions in the prescribed manner? Which of the two should be given preference? Service or the rosary?

GANDHI: Whatever the exigencies of service or adverse circumstances may be, Ramanama must not cease. The outward form will vary according to the occasion. The absence of the rosary does not interrupt Ramanama which has found an abiding place in the heart.

On one occasion Gandhi was asked whether mechanical repetition of prayers was not worse than useless, considering that it merely acted as an opiate on the soul. To that Gandhi replied that repetitions, when they were not mechanical, did produce marvellous results. He said, "Thus I do not regard the rosary as a superstition. It is an aid to the pacification of a wandering brain." For all his insistence on reciting *Ramanama*, cynics abounded. In one of his last references to the subject in *Harijan*, he averred: "I must repeat for the thousandth time that Ramanama is one of the many names for God. Ramanama is not an idle chant. It is conceived as a mode of addressing the all-pervasive God known to me, as to millions of Hindus, by the familiar name of Ramanama."

When a correspondent wrote to him suggesting that there were three aids to self-control of which two were outward and one, reciting *Ramanama*, was inward, Gandhi readily agreed. He wrote: "There is no doubt that Ramanama is the surest aid. If recited from the heart it charms away every evil thought, and evil thought gone, no corresponding action is possible." Gandhi pointed out that outward aids were all useless if the mind was weak. They were superfluous if the mind was pure. *Nama japa*, he insisted, cleansed the heart.

4

UNITY OF ALL RELIGIONS

In his biography of Gandhi, Penderel Moon notes that while Gandhi was in South Africa he had many Christian friends whose sincerity in the practice of their faith he came greatly to appreciate. He even had long discussions with them. He read the books on Christianity that his friends provided him, some of which seemed to him to support Hinduism. The one book that made the deepest impression on him was Leo Tolstoy's *The Kingdom of God is Within You*. His Christian friends made every effort to persuade Gandhi to embrace Christianity but though influenced by it, Gandhi could never accept it "as a perfect or the greatest religion". Gandhi also read the Koran and made a study of Islam, and as he put it, the "mental churning" which started in Pretoria went on for some years. As the years went by he was drawn more and more towards Hinduism—his own religion, and was greatly influenced and guided by the Bhagavadgita.

Even as a child, Gandhi had felt the need of a scripture that would serve him as an unfailing guide through the trials and temptations of life. The Vedas, he felt, could not supply that need if only because learning them would require fifteen to sixteen years of hard study for which he was then not ready. But the Gita gave, within the compass of its seven hundred verses, the quintessence of all the Shastras and the Upanishads. Gandhi therefore learnt Sanskrit to be able to read the Gita in the original. In an address to students of the Kashi Vishwa Vidyalaya in 1934, he said:

> Today the *Gita* is not only my Bible or my Koran; it is more than that—it is my mother. I lost my earthly mother who gave me birth long ago; but this eternal mother has completely filled her place by my side ever since. She has never changed, she has never failed me. When I am in difficulty or distress, I seek refuge in her bosom. Often in the course of my struggle against untouchability, I am confronted with conflicting opinions delivered by doctors of learning. Some of them tell me that untouchability as it is practised today has no sanction in Hinduism and they bless my efforts to eradicate it; but there are some others who maintain that untouchability has been an essential part of Hinduism from the very beginning. Which authority should I follow under the circumstances? I feel absolutely at sea.

Gandhi said that the Vedas and the Smritis were of no avail to him. He then approached "the Mother" and said, "Mother, these learned pandits have put me in a predicament. Help me out of my perplexity." And the mother, he said, referring of course, to the Gita, told him, "The assurance held out by me in the ninth chapter is not meant for the Brahmanas only, but for the sinner and the outcaste, the downtrodden and the disinherited, too." He must have been referring to these lines from the Gita:

Samoham sarvabhuteshu na me deshyosti na priyah
Ye bhajanti tu maam bhakthya mayi te teshu chaapyaham
(Ch. IX, *Shloka* 29)

(Equally impartial am I to all beings. My love is ever the same. But they that worship me with devotion are in me and I too am in them.)

As also to another verse:

Maam hi Partha vyapaashritya yepi syuh paapayonayah
Striyo vaishyaastathaa shudrastepi yaanti paraam gatim
(Ch. IX, *Shloka* 32)

(For if they take refuge in me, O Partha, even those who may be of base origin, women, men of the artisan caste, and serfs too, attain the highest goal.)

And having said that, Gandhi went on, "But in order to be worthy of that promise, we must be obedient and devoted children of the Mother and not disobedient and disloyal children, who only make a pretence of devotion."

Gandhi said that many believed that the Gita was too difficult a work for the man-in-the-street to understand. That thinking was ill-founded. The Gita, he said, enabled the late Lokmanya (Bal Gangadhar Tilak), out of his encyclopaedic learning and study, to produce a monumental commentary. Gandhi added that if one found all eighteen chapters too difficult to negotiate then one could make a careful study of the first three only since they gave in a nutshell what was propounded in greater detail and from different angles in the remaining fifteen chapters. He further simplified this by stating that even these three chapters could be further epitomised in a few verses selected from these chapters, making it easily accessible to lay readers. Gandhi continued:

At three distinct places the *Gita* goes even further and exhorts us to leave alone all "isms" and take refuge in the Lord alone, and it will be seen how baseless is the charge that the message of the *Gita* is too subtle or complicated for lay minds to understand. The *Gita* is the universal Mother. She turns away nobody. Her door is wide open to anyone who knocks. A true votary of the *Gita* does not know what disappointment is. He ever dwells in perennial joy and peace that passeth understanding. But that peace and joy come not to the sceptic or to him who is proud of his intellect or learning. It is reserved only for the humble in spirit who brings to her worship a fullness of faith and an undivided singleness of mind. There never was a man who worshipped her in that spirit and went back disappointed.

On another occasion Gandhi noted that the theme of the Gita was actually contained in the second chapter and the way to carry out the message was to be found in the third chapter. He however clarified that this did not mean that the other chapters had less merit. Indeed, he said, every one of them had a merit of its own.

According to Gandhi, the second chapter, instead of teaching the rules of physical warfare, tells us how a perfected man is to be known. "Krishna of the *Gita* is perfection and right knowledge personified; but the picture is imaginary. That does not mean that Krishna, the adored of his people, never lived. But perfection is imagined. The idea of a perfect incarnation is an aftergrowth." In the matter of incarnation, Gandhi had specific views. In his own translation of the Gita in Gujarati, he wrote:

> In Hinduism, incarnation is ascribed to one who has performed some extraordinary service of mankind. All embodied life is in reality an incarnation of God, but it is not usual to consider every living being an incarnation. Future generations pay this

homage to one who, in his own generation, has been extraordinarily religious in his conduct. I can see nothing wrong in this procedure; it takes nothing from God's greatness, and there is no violence done to truth . . . He who is the most religiously behaved has most of the divine spark in him. It is in accordance with this train of thought that Krishna enjoys, in Hinduism, the status of the most perfect incarnation.

Continued Gandhi:

This belief in incarnation is a testimony of man's lofty spiritual ambition. Man is not at peace with himself till he had become like unto God. The endeavour to reach this state is the supreme, the only ambition worth having. And this is self-realization. This self-realization is the subject of the *Gita*, as it is of all scriptures. But its author surely did not write it to establish that doctrine. The object of the *Gita* appears to me to be that of showing the most excellent way to attain self-realization. That, which is to be found, more or less clearly, spread out here and there in Hindu religious books, has been brought out in the clearest possible language in the *Gita* even at the risk of repetition. That matchless remedy is renunciation of fruits of action.

Gandhi considered renunciation among the highest virtues and considered it to be the centre around which the Gita is woven. He described renunciation as "the central sun around which devotion, knowledge, and the rest revolve like planets". But then, shouldn't one work? If one did not work, what was the body meant for? Wrote Gandhi: "The body has been likened to a prison. There must be action where there is a body. No embodied being is exempted from labour. And yet all religions proclaim that it is possible for man, by treating the body as the temple of God, to attain freedom. Every action is tainted, be it ever so trivial. How can the body be made the temple of God?

In other words, how can one be free from action, i.e. from the taint of sin? The *Gita* has answered the question in decisive language: 'By desireless action; by renouncing fruits of action; by dedicating all activities to God i.e. by surrendering oneself to Him body and soul.'"

Karmajam buddhiyuktaa hi phalam tyaktvaa manishinah
Janmabandhavinirmuktaahaa padam gacchantyanaamayam
(Ch. II, *Shloka* 51)

(The intelligent ones, united to pure reason, renounce the fruit which action yieldeth. Freed from the bondage of rebirth, they attain the state which is free from all ills.)

Gandhi held that absence of desire, or renunciation did not come for the mere talking about it. It was not attained by an intellectual feat. It was attainable only by a constant heart-churn. Right knowledge was necessary for attaining renunciation—learned men possessed knowledge of a kind. They might recite the Vedas from memory yet they might be steeped in self-indulgence. In order that knowledge may not run riot, the author of the Gita had insisted on devotion accompanying it and had given it the first place. Knowledge without devotion might be like a misfire. Therefore, Gandhi said, the Gita tells us, "Have devotion, and knowledge will follow." That devotion is not mere lip-worship, it is wrestling with death. Gandhi insisted that the devotion required by the Gita was no "soft-hearted effusiveness". It certainly was not blind faith. The devotion of the Gita had the least to do with externals. A devotee might use rosaries or forehead marks, or could make offerings, but those things were no test of his devotion. He was the true devotee who was jealous of none, who was a fount of mercy, who was without egoism, who was selfless, who treated alike cold and heat, happiness and misery, who was ever-giving, who was always contented, whose resolutions were firm, who had dedicated mind and soul to God, who caused no dread, who was not afraid of others, who was free from exultation, sorrow and fear, who was pure, who was versed in action and yet remained unaffected by it, who renounced all fruits, good or bad, who treated friend and foe alike, who was untouched by respect or disrespect, who was not puffed up by praise, who did not go under when people spoke ill of him, who loved silence and solitude, and who had disciplined reason.

When asked about bhakti (devotion) Gandhi answered that the popular notion of it is soft-heartedness and the telling of beads. He derisively added that some *bhaktas* disdained to do even a loving service while telling beads and only allowed themselves to be interrupted for the purposes of eating and drinking, but never for grinding corn or nursing patients. But, Gandhi noted, the Gita says that no one attains his goal without action and even men like Janaka attained salvation through action. The Gita says, "If even I were lazily to cease working, the world would perish. How much more necessary then for the people at large to engage in action?"

While on the one hand, it was beyond dispute that action binds, on the other hand it was equally true that all living beings had to do some work, whether they would or not. Here all activity, mental or physical, was included in the term "action". Then how was one to be free form the bondage of action, even though one may be acting?

Gandhi replied to his own question. He said, "The manner in which the *Gita* has solved the problem is, to my knowledge, unique. The *Gita* says, 'Do your allotted work but renounce its fruit—be detached and work—have no desire for reward and work.'" That, according to Gandhi, was the definitive teaching of the Gita. "He who gives up action, falls. He who gives up only reward, rises."

But renunciation of fruit in no way meant indifference to result. In regard to every action, one must know the result that was expected to follow, the means thereto, and the capacity for it. He, who being thus equipped, was without the desire for the result and was yet wholly engrossed in the due fulfilment of the task before him, was said to have renounced the fruits of his action. Having said that, Gandhi wanted to make a clarification. He said, "Let no one consider renunciation to mean want of fruit for the renouncer. The *Gita* reading does not warrant such a meaning. Renunciation means absence of hankering after fruit. As a matter of fact, he who renounces reaps a thousand fold. The renunciation of the *Gita* is the acid test of faith. He who is ever brooding over result often loses nerve in the performance of his duty. He becomes impatient and then gives vent to anger and begins to do unworthy things; he jumps from action to action, never remaining faithful to any. He who broods over results is like a man given to objects of senses; he is ever distracted, he says goodbye to all scruples, everything is right in his estimation and he therefore resorts to means fair and foul to attain his end."

Gandhi said that the Gita taught that what cannot be followed on a day-to-day practice could not be called religion. On that basis, as he read the meaning of the Gita, "all acts that are incapable of being performed without attachment are taboo". Thinking along these lines, said Gandhi, he felt that in trying to enforce in one's life the central teaching of the Gita, one was bound to follow truth and ahimsa. As he put it, "When there is no desire for fruit, there is no temptation for untruth or *himsa*."

But Gandhi could see doubts arising in the minds of his readers, as was evident from the letters he received. Thus, if the Gita believed in ahimsa, and urged absence of desire, why did the author take a war-like illustration? Gandhi was aware that when the Gita was written, although people believed in ahimsa, wars were an accepted way of life, but nobody observed the contradiction between war and ahimsa. To this apparent contradiction, Gandhi had a somewhat ingenuous interpretation. He put it thus:

> In assessing the implications of renunciation of fruit, we are not required to probe the mind of the author of the *Gita* as to his limitations of Ahimsa and the like. Because a poet puts a particular truth before the world, it does not necessarily follow that he has known or worked out all its great consequences, or that having done so, he is able always to express them fully. In this perhaps lies the greatness of the poem and the poet. A poet's meaning is limitless. Like man, the meaning of great writings suffers evolution. On examining the history of languages, we notice that the meaning of important words has changed or expanded. This is true of the *Gita*. The author has himself extended the meanings of some of the current words. We are able to discover this even on a superficial examination. It is possible that in the age prior to that of the *Gita*, offering of animals in sacrifice was permissible. But there is not a trace of it in the sacrifice in the *Gita* sense. In the *Gita* continuous concentration on God is the king of sacrifices. The third chapter seems to show that sacrifice chiefly means body labour for service. The third and the fourth chapters read together will give us other meanings for sacrifice but never animal sacrifice.

This sounds like an apologia but that it isn't. Meanings of words do change over the years, and Gandhi, for instance, has taken note of the meaning of the word *sanyasa*. The *sanyasa* of the Gita, asserts Gandhi, will not tolerate complete cessation of all activity. The *sanyasa* of the Gita, as Gandhi understood it, was "all work and yet no work". Gandhi explains that according to the letter of the Gita, it is possible that warfare is consistent with renunciation of fruit. He concedes however that after forty years of unremitting endeavour to fully enforce the teaching of the Gita in his own life, he had come to the conclusion that perfect renunciation was impossible without perfect observance of ahimsa in every shape and form. There is space here for a good argument.

For all that, Gandhi writes: "The *Gita* is not an aphoristic work; it is a great religious poem. The deeper you dive into it, the richer the meanings you get. It being meant for the people at large, there is pleasing repetition. With every age the important words will carry new and expanded meanings. But its central teaching will never vary. The seeker is at liberty to extract from this treasure any meaning he likes so as to enable him to enforce in his life the central teaching."

Gandhi, for all his love and reverence for the Gita, was in a real dilemma. Krishna asks Arjuna to fight because fighting is Arjuna's dharma. But for Gandhi, violence in any form and for whatever reason was unacceptable. How could he possibly reconcile the two? Gandhi held that the Gita described, in the form of physical warfare, the duel that went on in the minds of men. He did not succeed in convincing many of his fans and followers. One of them, Canon Sheppard, wrote to him:

> I hold the view that independently of the context of the *Gita* and preliminary conversation between Arjuna and Shri Krishna, Hinduism does not stand decisively for non-violence in regard to organised invasion. It would be straining too much to interpret all our best scriptures in this way. Hinduism holds, no doubt, the spirit of compassion and love as the very highest duty for man. But it does not preach what you and the pacifists preach, and it is no good straining everything into an allegory for this object.

Canon Sheppard was indeed being logical and making a strong point. As Gandhi often stressed, the Gita was his Mother who helped him at all times. But there was no easy way to duck the issue raised by Sheppard. Nevertheless, Gandhi replied:

> I have admitted in my introduction to the *Gita* known as *Anasakti Yoga* that it is not a treatise on non-violence nor was it written to condemn war. Hinduism as is practised today or has been known to have ever been practised, has certainly not condemned war as I do. What, however, I have done is to put a new but natural and logical interpretation upon the whole teaching of the *Gita* and the spirit of Hinduism. Hinduism, not to speak of other religions, is ever evolving. It has no one scripture, like the Koran or the Bible. Its scriptures are also evolving and suffering addition. The *Gita* itself is an instance in point. It has given new meaning to Karma, *Sanyasa*, *Yajna* etc. It has breathed new life into Hinduism. It has given an original rule of conduct. Not that what the *Gita* has given was not implied in previous writings, but the *Gita* put these implications in a concrete shape.

He noted that what he had done was perfectly historical and he had followed in the footsteps of his forefathers. He pointed out that at one time his ancestors sacrificed animals to propitiate angry Gods. Their descendants—his less remote ancestors—read a different meaning into the word "sacrifice" and they taught that it was meant to be a sacrifice of our baser self to please not angry gods but the one living God within. He added, "I hold that the logical outcome of the teaching of the *Gita* is decidedly for peace at the price of life itself. It is the highest aspiration of the human species."

Gandhi, it would seem, was not sure he was going to convince Sheppard of his stand. So, to make his point, he first averred that both the Ramayana and the Mahabharata were "undoubtedly allegories as the internal evidence shows". Secondly, he argued that even if "most probably" the two epics dealt with "historical figures" that did not affect his proposition. As he insisted, each epic described "the eternal duel that goes on between the forces of darkness and of light". And finally, as if to clinch his argument, he added, "Anyway, I must disclaim any intention of straining the meaning of Hinduism or the *Gita* to suit any preconceived notions of mine. My notions were the outcome of the study of the *Gita*, Ramayana, Mahabharata, Upanishads, etc."

V. B. Kher, who edited Gandhi's thoughts in his classic study *The Essence of Hinduism*, reproduces a conversation between two questioners and Gandhi on this very topic. Doesn't Krishna recommend violence towards the end of the *Gita*, the questioners want to know?

GANDHI: I don't think so. I am also fighting. I should not be fighting effectively if I were fighting violently. The message of the *Gita* is to be found in the second chapter of the *Gita* where Krishna speaks of the balanced state of mind, of mental equipoise. In nineteen verses at the close of the second chapter of the *Gita*, Krishna explains how this state can be achieved. It can be achieved, he tells us, after killing all your passions. It is not possible to kill your brother after having killed all your passions. I should like to see that man dealing death—who has no passions, who is indifferent to pleasure and pain, who is undisturbed by the storms that trouble mortal man. The whole thing is described in a language of beauty that is unsurpassed. These verses show that the fight Krishna speaks of is a spiritual fight.

QUESTIONERS: To the common mind it sounds as though it was actual fighting.

GANDHI: You must read the whole thing dispassionately in its true context. After the first mention of fighting, there is no mention of fighting at all. The rest is a spiritual discourse.

QUESTIONERS: Has anybody interpreted it like you?

GANDHI: Yes. The fight is there, but the fight as it is going on within. The Pandavas and Kauravas are the forces of good and evil within. The war is the war between Jekyll and Hyde, God and Satan, going on in the human breast. The internal evidence in support of this interpretation is there in the work itself and in the Mahabharata of which the *Gita* is a minute part. It is not a history of war between two families but the history of man—the history of the spiritual struggle of man.

QUESTIONERS: Is the central teaching of the *Gita* selfless action or non-violence?

GANDHI: I have no doubt that it is *anasakti*selfless action. Indeed I have called my little translation of the *Gita Anasakti Yoga*. And *anasakti* transcends ahimsa. He who would be *anasakta* (selfless) has necessarily to practise non-violence in order to attain the state of selflessness. *Ahimsa* is therefore a necessary preliminary, it is included in *anasakti*, it does not go beyond it.

QUESTIONERS: Then does the *Gita* teach *himsa* and ahimsa both?

GANDHI: I do not read that meaning in the *Gita*. It is quite likely that the author did not write to inculcate ahimsa but as a commentary draws innumerable interpretations from a poetic text, even so, I interpret the *Gita* to mean that if its central theme is *anasakti*, it also teaches ahimsa. Whilst we are in the flesh and tread the solid earth, we have to practise ahimsa. In the life beyond, there is *himsa* or ahimsa.

QUESTIONERS: But Lord Krishna actually counters the doctrine of ahimsa. For Arjuna utters this pacifist resolve:
Better I deem it if my kinsmen strike
To face them weaponless, and bare my breast
To shaft and spear, than answer blow with blow.
And Lord Krishna teaches him to answer "blow with blow".

GANDHI: There I join issue with you. Those words of Arjuna were words of pretentious wisdom. "Until yesterday," says Krishna to him, "you fought your kinsmen with deadly weapons without the slightest compunction. Even today you would strike if the enemy was a stranger and not your kith and kin." The question before him was not of non-violence but whether he should slay his nearest and dearest.

The question that often arises is why Gandhi, like Ashoka, did not follow the precepts of the Buddha with whose ahimsa ideology he had so much in common. Strange though it may sound, there are very few references to the Buddha in the many talks and pages of writings that Gandhi indulged in, in his defence of ahimsa and non-violence. It is not that Gandhi did not have a high opinion of him or had not studied Buddhism. As he wrote in *Harijan*: "I have the greatest veneration for the Buddha. He is one of the greatest preachers of peace. The gospel of the Buddha is the gospel of love."

As a matter of fact, many in his day "accused" him of spreading Buddhism and teaching it under the guise of *sanatana* Hinduism. It did not affect Gandhi. On the contrary he felt proud of being accused of being a follower of the Buddha. In a speech he delivered in Sri Lanka in 1927, he admitted that he owed "a great deal to the inspiration" that he derived from the life of the Enlightened One. He said Gautama was himself a "Hindu of Hindus" and gave life to some of the teachings that were buried in the Vedas and which were overgrown with weeds. Said Gandhi, "His great Hindu spirit cut its way through the forest of words, meaningless words, which had overlaid the golden truth that was in the Vedas. He made some of the words of the Vedas yield a meaning to which the men of his generation were utter strangers, and he found in India the most congenial soil."

Gandhi said that wherever the Buddha went he was followed by and surrounded not by non-Hindus, but Hindus, those who were themselves saturated with the Vedic law. But the Buddha's teaching, like his heart, was all-expanding and all-embracing. "At the risk of being called a follower of the Buddha," Gandhi said, "I claim this achievement as a triumph of Hinduism. Buddha never rejected Hinduism but he broadened its base. He gave it a new life and a new interpretation."

Gandhi said that he often heard that Buddha did not believe in God. He told his listeners, "In my humble opinion the confusion has arisen over his rejection and just rejection of all the base things that passed in his generation under the name of God . . . His whole soul rose in mighty indignation against the belief that a being called God required for his satisfaction the living blood of animals in order that he might be pleased, animals who were his own creation." Gandhi said that in the circumstances Buddha re-instated God in the right place and dethroned the usurper who, for the time being, seemed happy to occupy the White Throne. And he added: "He emphasized and re-declared the eternal and unalterable existence of the moral government of this universe. He unhesitatingly said that the law was God Himself."

Gandhi wanted to discourage the strong belief that Gautama, the Buddha, did not believe in God. He said, "God's laws are eternal and unalterable and not separable from God Himself. It is an indispensable condition of His very perfection." It was that, said Gandhi, that led to the misunderstanding that Buddha disbelieved in God and simply believed in the moral law. And because of this, there arose the confusion about the proper understanding of the great word "nirvana". Gandhi insisted that nirvana is undoubtedly not utter extinction. As far as he was able to understand the central fact of Buddha's life, nirvana is utter extinction of all that is base in us, all that is vicious in us, all that is corrupt and corruptible in us. Nirvana is not the black dead peace of the grave, but the living peace, the living happiness of a soul which is conscious of itself and conscious of having found its own abode in the heart of the Eternal.

Expressing his own assessment of Buddhism he said that it was his "deliberate opinion" that the essential part of the teachings of the Buddha now forms a part of Hinduism. He said, "It is impossible to Hindu India today to retrace her steps and go beyond the great reformation that Gautama effected in Hinduism. By his immense sacrifice, by his great renunciation and by immaculate purity of his life he left an indelible impression on Hinduism and Hinduism owes an eternal debt of gratitude to that great teacher . . . what Hinduism did not assimilate of what passes as Buddhism today was not an essential part of the Buddha's life and his teachings."

According to Gandhi his "fixed opinion" was that Buddhism, or rather the teaching of the Buddha, found its full fruition in India and it could not be otherwise, for Gautama was himself a Hindu of Hindus. Gandhi said his Buddha was "saturated with the best that was in Hinduism, and he gave life to some of the teachings that were buried in the Vedas which were overgrown with weeds".

"Great as the Buddha's contribution to humanity was in restoring God to his eternal place," Gandhi said, "greater still was his contribution to humanity in his exacting regard for all life, be it ever so low."

It should become apparent to anyone who has read Gandhi or has read on him that the one all-absorbing subject he was never tired of talking or writing about was God. It was not that he was imposing his views on anyone but he was constantly questioned on the subject. Happily for him, throughout his life he edited a weekly in which he could express his views freely and frankly.

Thus, on one occasion, a young man earnestly wrote to Gandhi: "You have mentioned in your article [in *Harijan*] of a *living* faith in a *living* God. I shall feel highly gratified, and I think you will be rendering a great benefit to the young world, if you put forth some positive, undeniable proofs of the existence of God. I have the confidence that you will no more mystify the already mystified problem and will throw some definite light on the subject."

That was indeed a challenging poser. But Gandhi did not hesitate to reply. He was of the view that most people did have a living faith in a living God. For them, he said, "it is". He felt that belief in God had to be based on faith which transcends reason, for God was beyond the senses. He conceded that what he wrote "will not remove the mist to which the correspondent alludes". Having said that, he continued:

The writer supposes that I might have realized the existence of a living God. I can lay no such claim. But I do have a living faith in a living God even as I have a living faith in many things that scientists tell me. It may be retorted that what the scientists say can be verified if one followed the prescription given for realizing the facts which are taken for granted. Precisely in that manner speak the Rishis and the Prophets. They say anybody following the path they have trodden can realize God.

Gandhi said that the fact is "we do not want to follow the path leading to realization and we wont take the testimony of eye witnesses about the one thing that really matters. Not all the achievements of physical sciences put together can compare with that which gives us a living faith in God."

He said, "Those who do not want to believe in the existence of God do not believe in the existence of anything apart from the body... For such persons the weightiest argument in proof of the existence of soul or God is of no avail. You cannot make a person who has stuffed his ears, listen to, much less appreciate, the finest music. Even so can you not convince those about existence of a living God who do not want the conviction." Then, with more passion than one expects from him, Gandhi wrote:

> Are all the scriptures of the world old women's tales of superstition? Is the testimony of the Rishis, the Prophets to be rejected? Is the testimony of Chaitanya, Ramakrishna Paramhamsa, Tukaram, Dnyandeva, Ramdas, Nanak, Kabir, Tulasidas of no value? What about Ramamohan Roy, Devendranath Tagore, Vivekananda—all modern men as well educated as the tallest among the living ones? I omit the living witnesses whose evidence would be considered unimpeachable. This belief in God has to be based on faith which transcends reason.

Gandhi was confronted in his lifetime by votaries of Hinduism and Islam with scriptural authority in support of certain practices which appeared to be repugnant to his conscience and were against trained reason, universal justice, and general humanity. In such cases his stand was unambiguous and clear. For example, when extracts from scriptures were cited by Hindu orthodoxy in support of untouchability, Gandhi rejected such authority in no uncertain terms.

> Let us not deceive ourselves into the belief that everything that is written in Sanskrit and printed in Shastras has any binding effect on us. That which is opposed to the fundamental maxims of morality, that which is opposed to trained reason, cannot be claimed as Shastra no matter how ancient it may be.

Again, he observed, "I have no hesitation in rejecting scriptural authority of a doubtful character in order to support a sinful institution. Indeed I would reject scriptural authority if it is in conflict with sober reason or the dictates of the heart. Authority sustains and ennobles the weak when it is the handwork of reason but it degrades them when it supplants reason sanctified by the still small voice within."

To Gandhi, morals, ethics, and religion were convertible terms. Hence he declared categorically that as soon as we lose the moral basis we cease to be religious. Man, for instance, cannot be untruthful, cruel, or incontinent and claim to have God on his side. Similarly, the punishment of stoning to death for apostasy was defended on the ground of its mention in the Koran by certain Muslim clerics. In response to a personal appeal made to Gandhi to express his opinion on the subject, he wrote:

> As a human being living in the fear of God I should question the morality of the method under any circumstance whatsoever. Whatever may have been necessary or permissible during the

> Prophet's lifetime and in that age, this particular form of penalty cannot be defended on the mere ground of its mention in the Koran. Every formula of every religion has in this age of reason, to submit to the acid test of reason and universal justice if it is to ask for universal assent. Error can claim no exemption even if it can be supported by the scriptures of the world . . . It is the form of penalty that wounds the human conscience. Both reason and heart refuse to reconcile themselves to torture for any crime, no matter how vile the crime may be.

Gandhi argued that complete realisation of God was impossible in this embodied life. Nor was it necessary. A living, immoveable faith was all that was required for reaching the full spiritual height attainable by human beings. God was not outside "this earthly course of ours". So, argued Gandhi, exterior proof was not of much avail, if any at all. He said, "We must ever fail to perceive Him through the senses, because He is beyond them. We can feel Him, if we will but withdraw ourselves from the senses. The divine music is incessantly going on within ourselves, but the loud senses drown the delicate music which is unlike and infinitely superior to anything we can perceive or hear with our senses." Rising to even greater heights, Gandhi continued:

> The writer wants to know why, if God is a God of mercy and justice, He allows all the miseries and sorrows we see around us. I can give no satisfactory explanation. He imputes to me a sense of defeat and humiliation. I have no such sense of defeat, humiliation or despair. My retirement, such as it is, has nothing to do with any defeat. It is no more and no less than a course of self-purification and self-preparation . . . It may be that what we mistake as sorrows, injustices and the like are not such in truth. If we could solve all the mysteries of the universe, we would be co-equals with God. Every drop of the ocean shares its glory but is not the ocean. Realizing our littleness during this tiny span of life, we close every morning prayer

with the recitation of a verse which means: "Misery so-called is no misery nor riches so-called riches. Forgetting (or denying) God is the true misery, remembering (or faith in) God is true riches."

In his early years Gandhi had read a great deal of Christianity, especially during his years in South Africa, thanks to many Christian friends he had come across. He respected Christianity, as he did Islam, but he was to say, "For me Hinduism is all-sufficing. Every variety of belief finds protection in its ample fold."

As he made it clear, Hinduism is not an exclusive religion. There was room in it for worship of all the prophets in the world. It was not a missionary religion in the ordinary sense of the term. It had no doubt absorbed many tribes in its fold, but that absorption had been of an evolutionary, imperceptible character. Hinduism told everyone to worship God according to one's own faith or dharma, and so it had lived at peace with all religions. As early as 1921, he wrote in *Young India*:

> The chief value of Hinduism lies in holding the actual belief that *all* life (not only human beings, but all sentient beings) is one, i.e. all life coming from the one universal source, call it Allah, God or Parameshwara.
>
> My Hinduism is not sectarian. It includes all that I know to be the best in Islam, Christianity, Buddhism and Zoroastrianism . . . Truth is my religion and ahimsa is the only way of its realization. I have rejected once and for all the doctrine of the sword.

Further he wrote:

> Hinduism with its message of ahimsa is the most glorious religion in the world—as my wife is to me the most beautiful

woman in the world—but others may feel the same about their own religion.

Gandhi asserted that Hinduism's definitive contribution to Indian culture was ahimsa. That, said Gandhi, has given a definite bias to the history of the country for the last hundred years and over and it has not ceased to be a living force in the lives of India's millions to this day.

As has been said often enough, Gandhi had read widely on Christianity. As he put it, "There is nothing in the world that would keep me from professing Christianity or any other faith, the moment I felt the truth of and the need for it." He wrote:

> Where there is fear there is no religion . . . If I could call myself, say, a Christian or a Mussalman, with my own interpretation of the Bible or the Koran, I should not hesitate to call myself either. For then Hindu, Christian and Mussalman would be synonymous terms. I do not believe that in the other world there are either Hindus, nor Christians nor Mussalmans. They all are judged not according to their labels, or professions, but according to their actions, irrespective of their professions. During our earthly existence there will always be these labels. I, therefore, prefer to retain the label of my forefathers, so long as it does not cramp my growth and does not debar me from assimilating all that is good anywhere else.

Gandhi said that though he admired much in Christianity, he was unable to identify himself with orthodox Christianity. Hinduism, as he knew it, entirely satisfied his soul. It filled his whole being and he found solace in the Gita and the Upanishads that he missed even in the Sermon on the Mount. He said that it was not that he did not prize the ideal presented therein. Not that some of the precious teachings of the Sermon on the Mount had not left a deep impression on him. "But," he said, "when doubts haunt me, when disappointments stare me in the face, and when I see not one ray of light on the horizon, I turn to the *Bhagavadgita* and find a verse to comfort me; and I immediately begin to smile in the midst of overwhelming sorrow. My life has been full of external tragedies and if they have not left any visible and indelible effect on me, I owe it to the teachings of the *Bhagavadgita*."

It is remarkable what Gandhi had to say about both Christianity and Islam as long ago as 1920-21. Let it be remembered that this was not long after the First World War (1914-1918). Speaking then of Christianity, Gandhi said, "It is my firm opinion that Europe today represents not the spirit of God or Christianity, but the spirit of Satan. And Satan's successes are the greatest when he appears with the name of God on his lips. Europe is today only nominally Christian . . . It is a very curious commentary on the West that although it professes Christianity, there is no Christianity or Christ in the West . . . Christianity became disfigured when it went to the West. I am sorry to have to say that."

Gandhi had a request to make to his Christian brethren. He told them not to take their Christianity as it is interpreted in the West "with her blood-stained fingers" where people were fighting with "one another as never before". Gandhi noted that "the indirect influence of Christianity has been to quicken Hinduism into life". He also refused to ascribe "exclusive divinity" to Jesus. Jesus, he said, was as divine as Krishna or Rama or Mohammed or Zoroaster. Gandhi even went further to say that he did not regard "every word of the Bible as the inspired word of God", even as he did not regard every word of the Vedas or the Koran as inspired. "The sum total of these books," he went on, "is certainly inspired, but I miss that inspiration in many of the things taken individually." However, he added, "Though I cannot claim to be a Christian in the sectarian sense, the example of Jesus' suffering is a factor in the composition of my undying faith in non-violence which rules all my actions, worldly and temporal."

Gandhi said that to him Jesus meant "one of the greatest teachers humanity has ever had". And he asked, "To His believers, he was God's only begotten Son. Could the fact that I do or do not accept this belief make Jesus have any more or less influence in my life? Is all the grandeur of His teaching and of His doctrine to be forbidden to me? I cannot believe so."

Gandhi said that it was impossible to estimate the merits of the various religions of the world and it was unnecessary and harmful even to attempt it. There was much ignorance and superstition in India but deep down among Indians was a faith in God. Said Gandhi, "If Muhammad came to India today, he would disown many of his so-called followers and own me as a true Muslim, as Jesus would own me as a true Christian."

Gandhi's remarks on Islam merit attention. For one thing, he said that he regarded Islam to be a religion of peace in the same sense as Christianity, Buddhism, and Hinduism. No doubt there were differences in degree, he said, but the object of these religions was peace. In his early writings, Gandhi reminded his readers that he had read the Koran more than once because his religion enabled him and obliged him to imbibe all that was good in all the religions of the world. He clarified that he wrote about Islam with the same care of its prestige as Hinduism.

He went on, "There is nothing in the Koran to warrant the use of force for conversion. The Holy Book says in the clearest language possible, that 'there is no compulsion in religion'." Gandhi felt that the Prophet's whole life was a repudiation of compulsion in religion. And he summed up his views thus:

Islam would cease to be a world religion if it were to rely on force for its propagation. I have given my opinion that the followers of Islam are too free with the sword. But that is not due to the teaching of the Koran. This is due in my opinion to the environment in which Islam was born. Christianity has a bloody record against it, not because Jesus was found wanting, but because the environment in which it spread was not responsive to his lofty teaching . . .

I have come to the conclusion that the teaching of the Koran is essentially in favour of non-violence. Non-violence is better than violence, it is said in the Koran. Non-violence is enjoined as a duty; violence is permitted as a necessity.

Rev. Jesudasan's comments on Gandhi's approach to Christ and Christianity are very pertinent. He writes:

To affirm Gandhi's faith in Christ is not to claim Gandhi for Christianity nor is it merely to see the full meaning of Christ through Gandhi. Through his existential identification with the God of suffering and saving love, Gandhi passes into the redeeming reality of the incarnation, opening and showing us the way to do the same . . . In accepting the depths of human weakness Gandhi made the power of God manifest, as Jesus had before him.

As Rev. Jesudasan understood Gandhi's approach to Christianity, Gandhi did not reinforce Christian dogma but went beyond it to embrace Christian morality. Miracles did not interest Gandhi as apology or proof. Actually upon his first reading of the Bible Gandhi was repelled by the literal meaning of many Biblical texts, refusing to take them as the Word of God. In evaluating all Scriptures, Gandhi's criterion was morality—not sectarian, but universal morality. If religions gave conflicting counsel, Gandhi applied three criteria by which to discriminate among them: the superiority of truth over everything that conflicted with it; rejection of everything that conflicted with non-violence; and, on things that could be reasoned out, rejection of everything that conflicted with reason. Thus, Rev. Jesudasan pointed out, that which reconciled Gandhi to any teaching of Christ, was not his alleged miracles, but the conformity of his teaching with Gandhi's criteria of universal morality.

Noted Rev. Jesudasan: "Gandhi believed that Jesus had attained the highest degree of perfection possible for a person, given the limitations of the flesh. He discounted miracles." He quoted Gandhi as saying:

> I believe in the perfectibility of human nature. Jesus came as near to perfection as possible. To say that he was perfect is to deny God's superiority to man . . . Being necessarily limited by the bonds of flesh, we can attain perfection only after the dissolution of the body. Therefore God alone is absolutely perfect. When He descends to earth, He of His own accord limits Himself. Jesus died on the Cross because he was limited by the flesh. I do not need either the prophecies or the miracles to establish Jesus' greatness as a teacher. Nothing can be more miraculous than the three years of his ministry . . . I do not deny that Jesus had certain psychic powers and he was undoubtedly filled with the love of humanity. But he brought to life not people who were dead but who were believed to be dead. The laws of Nature are changeless, unchangeable, and there are no miracles in the sense of infringement or interruption of Nature's laws. But we limited beings fancy all kinds of things and impute our limitations to God. We may copy God, but not He us.

Gandhi had no trouble affirming the perfection of Jesus at the moment of his death on the cross but he had his questions in locating that great virtue during Jesus' lifetime. Thus, when asked about the worship of "incarnations" that were historical figures, Gandhi said:

Christians worship Christ who was resurrected. In the same manner those who worship Rama and Krishna worship Rama and Krishna who are more living than you are or certainly more living than I am. They live now and will live until eternity . . . I worship the living Rama and Krishna, the incarnation of all that is True and Good and Perfect.

Why did Gandhi worship Krishna? Writing in *Anasakti Yoga*, Gandhi had said:

In Hinduism, incarnation is ascribed to one who has performed some extraordinary service of mankind. All embodied life is in reality an incarnation of God, but it is not usual to consider every living being as an incarnation. Future generations pay this homage to one who, in his own generation, has been extraordinarily religious in his conduct. I can see nothing wrong in this procedure; it takes nothing from God's greatness and there is no violence done to truth. There is an Urdu saying which means: Adam is not God but he is the spark of the Divine. And therefore, he who is most religiously behaved has most of the divine spark in him. It is in accordance with this train of thought that Krishna enjoys in Hinduism the status of the most perfect incarnation. The belief in incarnation is a testimony to man's lofty spiritual ambition. Man is not at peace with himself till he has become like unto God. The endeavour to reach this state is the supreme, the only ambition, worth having. And this is self-realisation. This self-realisation is the subject of the *Gita*, as it is of all scriptures.

There is something deeply touching in Gandhi's total faith in God as he saw him. In all the change that he perceived around him he could see a "living power that is changeless, that holds together, that creates, dissolves and recreates". He described that informing power or spirit as God in some of the most beautiful and profound language: "Since nothing else I see merely through the senses can or will persist, He alone is. And is this power benevolent or malevolent? I see it purely as benevolent. For I can see that in the midst of death, life persists, in the midst of untruth, truth persists, in the midst of darkness light persists. Hence I gather that God is Life, Truth, and Light. He is Love. He is the Supreme Good." Only, he added, "He is no God who merely satisfies the intellect, if He ever does. God to be God has to rule the heart and transform it . . . Exercise of faith will be the safest where there is a clear determination summarily to reject all that is contrary to Truth and Love."

And since, he said, faith itself cannot be proved by extraneous evidence, the safest course is to believe in the moral government of the world and therefore in the supremacy of the moral law, the law of truth and love.

There was no end to people wishing to ask Gandhi what Hinduism meant to him. But Gandhi never shirked from answering questions howsoever embarrassing or provocative they sounded. An American professor in comparative Theology, on a visit to India to study Indian religions, asked Gandhi to briefly explain the essence of Hinduism as she had been told that "Gandhi was the life and soul of Hinduism". "It is hardly wise," she said, "to rest content to teach what you can out of books. One must meet the true representatives of these living religions." Gandhi did not disappoint her. He told her that the chief value of Hinduism lay in holding the actual belief that *all* life is one. There is in Hinduism, Gandhi said, a scripture called *Vishnusahasranama* which meant one thousand names of God. These one thousand names, he said, did not mean that God is limited to those names, but that he had as many names as one could possibly give him. Said Gandhi, "You may give Him as many names as you like, provided it is one God without a second, whose name you are invoking." That also meant, added Gandhi, that he was nameless. And he went on:

> This unity of *all* life is a peculiarity of Hinduism which confines salvation not to human beings alone but says that it is possible for all God's creatures. It may be that it is not possible, save through the human form, but that does not make man the lord of creation. It makes him the servant of God's creation.

The nature of the question asked kept changing but there always was a certain curiosity as to what Gandhi thought on a given issue. On another occasion, a correspondent, styling himself as a *sanatani* Hindu, wanted to know from Gandhi how he would describe a *sanatanist*, considering that "every Hindu regards his own personal usage as the *sanatani* usage". Gandhi did not hesitate to provide his answer. Hinduism, he pointed out, was a living organism, liable to growth and decay and subject to the laws of nature. One and indivisible at the root, Hinduism grew into a vast tree with innumerable branches. The changes in the seasons affected it. It had its autumn and summer, its winter and spring. The rains nourished it and fructified it too. It was, and was not, based on scriptures. It did not derive its authority from one book. The Gita was universally accepted but even then it only showed the way. It had hardly any effect on custom. Hinduism was like the Ganga, pure and unsullied at its source but taking in its course the impurities in the way. Custom, Gandhi pointed out, is not religion. Custom may change but religion remained unaltered.

He added, "Purity of Hinduism depends on the self-restraint of its votaries. Whenever their religion has been in danger, the Hindus have undergone rigorous penance, searched the causes of the danger and devised means for combating them. The Shastras are ever growing. The Vedas, Upanishads, Smritis, Puranas and Itihasas did not arise at one and the same time. Each grew out of the necessities of particular periods, and therefore, they seem to conflict with one another."

Gandhi said that Hinduism was a living organism that could flourish and deteriorate but it abhorred stagnation. Knowledge was limitless and so also the application of truth. "Every day," he said, "we add to our knowledge of the powers of Atman, and we shall keep on doing so. New experience will teach us new duties, but truth shall ever be the same."

On another occasion he was asked why he was a Hindu! He said that being born in a Hindu family, he had remained a Hindu. But then he added:

I should reject it, if I found it inconsistent with my moral sense or my spiritual growth. On examination I have found it to be the most tolerant of all religions known to me. Its freedom from dogma makes a forcible appeal to me in as much as it gives the votary the largest scope for self-expression. Not being an exclusive religion, it enables the followers of that faith not merely to respect all the other religions, but it also enables them to admire and assimilate whatever may be good in the other faiths. Non-violence is common to all religions, but it has found the highest expression and application in Hinduism. (I do not regard Jainism or Buddhism as separate from Hinduism.) Hinduism believes in the oneness not of merely all human life but in the oneness of all that lives. Its worship of the cow is, in my opinion, its unique contribution to the evolution of humanitarianism. It is a practical application of the belief in the oneness and, therefore, sacredness, of all life. The great belief in transmigration is a direct consequence of that belief. Finally the discovery of the law of Varnashrama is a magnificent result of the ceaseless search for truth."

It is remarkable that in the *Hutchinson Helicon Encyclopaedia of Living Faiths*, edited by R. Zachner, in the section on Hinduism contributed by Prof. A L. Basham, he should have found it necessary to conclude with a very significant and powerfully apt quote from Gandhi. He states:

It [Hinduism] will survive, continuing to change with changing conditions, its plasticity allowing it to adapt itself to fresh situations and yet in some sense to remain true to the Ancient Wisdom. The words of Mahatma Gandhi with their paradoxical and typically Indian identification of true progress and return to the starting point might well be the words of Mother India herself. Said Gandhi: "Consider my spinning wheel. A full turn of the wheel is called a revolution. The revolution of the stars is a revolution of light, that of the seasons, of fruit and flower. A revolution in man's history should be of justice and goodness. Those who want to mock me and spinning wheel say: 'You want to put the clock back.' No my friends, I am the most advanced revolutionary, and I need only let the clock go on for it to come back to the starting point of its own accord.

"A revolution is a return to the First Principle, to the Eternal. Some men cling to the forms of the past and the memory of the dead and they live like the dead. Others hurl themselves into foolish novelties until they plunge into the void. I go forward without losing my way, for I am always coming back to the most ancient traditions through a complete revolution, a total but natural reversal willed by God and coming at its appointed time."

What is this *varnashrama* that Gandhi talks about? And what is *varnashramadharma*? Navajivan Publishing House once published in book form all of Gandhi's views on these two subjects in Gujarati, to which Gandhi provided an introduction. These were later translated into English by his devoted secretary, Mahadev Desai.

In the first place Gandhi noted that the words varna and ashrama are rarely used in separation and the compound word *varnashramadharma* was familiar to all Hindus. Indeed, he said, Hinduism is but another word, though imperfect, for *varnashramadharma*. The dharma (religion or law) that Hindus have professed to observe, he noted, is *varnashramadharma*. But to say that the dharma of the Hindus is Aryan did not carry one very far. Hinduism was nothing without the law of varna and ashrama. It would be impossible to find any Smriti work of which a large part was not devoted to *varnashramadharma*. Gandhi said that so far as the law of ashrama is concerned, it is extinct, alike in profession and observance. Hinduism laid down four ashramas or stages—the life of a *brahmachari* (continent student), the life of a *grihastha* (householder), the life of a *vanaprastha* (one who has retired), and the life of a *sanyasi* (one who has renounced)—through which every Hindu had to pass to fulfil his purpose in life. However, Gandhi said, the first and third stages, of *brahmacharya* and *vanaprastha*, are practically non-existent today, and the fourth, *sanyasa*, was observed only in name, not in spirit.

As Gandhi saw it, *grihasthas* or householders were all of a kind, in as much as they ate and drank, and like all created beings, propagated their kind. But in doing so they only fulfilled the law of the flesh and not of the spirit. Only those married couples who fulfilled the law of the spirit could be said to observe the law of *grihasthashrama*. Those who lived the mere animal life did not observe the law. The lives of householders, as then lived, was one of indulgence. And as the four stages represented a ladder of growth and were interdependent, one could not leap to the stage of *vanaprastha* or *sanyasa* unless he or she fulfilled the law of the first two ashramas—*brahmacharya* and *grihastha*. As Gandhi saw life then around him, the law of the ashrama therefore was a "dead letter". He added:

> Varna can certainly be said to exist, though in a distorted form. There are four Varnas, but the distortion that passes as Varna today is divided into countless castes. All the four Varnas are divided into numerous castes and sub-castes, but whilst those

who belong to the first three are not ashamed to declare that they belong to them, those who belong to the fourth, viz., Shoodra, prefer to declare the sub-caste as their label rather than their Varna which they regard as a badge of humiliation.

Gandhi insisted that a label never revealed a man's true character nor did the fact that a man clung to it show that he deserved it. One did not become a Brahmin by calling himself a Brahmin. Not until a man revealed in his life the attributes of a Brahmin could he deserve that name. The law was the law of one's being, which one had to fulfil. And the fulfilment had to be spontaneous and not a matter of honour and shame. Gandhi warned: "Let no one contend that Varna exists today, because all the functions of the different Varnas are being performed by someone or other and somehow or other. Varna is intimately, if not indissolubly, connected with birth, and the observance of the law of Varna means the following on the part of us all the hereditary and traditional calling of our forefathers in a spirit of duty."

Varna, said Gandhi, is determined by birth but can be retained only by observing its obligations. One born of Brahmin parents would be called a Brahmin but if his life failed to reveal the attributes of a Brahmin when he came of age, could not be called a Brahmin. On the other hand, one born in another caste would be eligible to be a Brahmin if his conduct merited it. And he added, "Varna thus conceived is no man-made institution but the law of life universally governing the human family. Fulfilment of the law would make life liveable, would spread peace and content, end all clashes and conflicts, put an end to starvation and pauperization, solve the problem of population, and even end disease and suffering."

And he quoted the Buddha as saying, "Neither matted hair, nor noble birth, nor caste make a Brahmana. The man of Truth and Law is the Brahmana." As the Gita itself said:

Chaaturvarnyam mayaa srushtam gunakarmavibhaagashah
Tasya kartaaramapi maam viddhyakartaaramavyayam
(Ch. IV, *Shloka* 13)

(The order of the four varnas was created by me according to the different qualities and actions of each. Although I am the creator thereof, know me as non-doer and immutable.)

Gandhi said that in the true conception of the law of varna, no one is superior to any other. All occupations are equal and honourable in so far as they are not in conflict with morals, private or public. A scavenger has the same status as a Brahmin. Was it not Max Mueller, Gandhi asked, who said that it was in Hinduism more than in any other religion that life was no more and no less than duty? Gandhi conceded that there was no doubt that at some stages of its evolution, Hinduism suffered corruption, and the canker of superiority and inferiority entered and vitiated it. "But this notion of inequality," he said, "seems to me wholly against the spirit of sacrifice which dominates everything in Hinduism." And he added: "There is no room for arrogation of superiority by one class over another in a scheme of life based on Ahimsa whose active form is undefiled love for all life."

Gandhi called the Gita his Mother. It answered all his difficulties and was his *Kamadhenu*, his guide, his open sesame "in hundred of moments of doubt and difficulty". He swore that he could not recall a single occasion when the Gita failed him. But addressing in 1936 an audience in Travancore, he said that he had come across a mantra that had totally captivated him. "I have now come to the final conclusion that if all the Upanishads and all the other scriptures happened all of a sudden to be reduced to ashes and if only the first verse in the *Ishopanishad* were left intact in the memory of Hindus, Hinduism would live for ever." And what is this verse?

> *Ishavasyamidham sarvam yatkincha jagatyam jagat*
> *Thena thyakthena bhunjithaa ma gridha kasyasviddhanam*

Gandhi sought to explain what these four glorious lines meant. His explanation was as follows: "All this that we see in this great universe is pervaded by God. Renounce it and enjoy it!" But there was more to it, especially when the mantra said: "Do not covet anybody's wealth or possession." With becoming passion Gandhi spoke at a public meeting in Quilon:

> As I read the *mantra* in the light of the *Gita*, or the *Gita* in the light of the *mantra*, I find that the *Gita* is a commentary on this *mantra*. It seems to be to satisfy the cravings of the Socialist and the Communist, of the philosopher and the economist. I venture to suggest to all who do not belong to the Hindu faith that it satisfies their cravings also. And if it is true—and I hold it to be true—you need not take anything in Hinduism which is inconsistent with or contrary to the meaning of this *mantra*. What more can a man in the street want to learn than this that the one God and Creator and Master of all that lives pervades the universe?... If you believe that God pervades everything that He has created, you must believe that you cannot enjoy anything that is not given by Him.

The next day, addressing another meeting, this time at Haripad, Gandhi returned to the same subject with even more passion. He said, "Let there be renunciation in the spirit of *Krishnarpanamastusarvam*. Every day in the morning, everyone who believes in Bhagavatdharma has to dedicate his thoughts, words and deeds to Krishna, and not until he has performed that daily act of renunciation or dedication has he the right of touching anything or drinking even a cup of water." His final speech in Travancore in 1937 was at Kottayam when he returned to the *Ishopanishad*. It was even more passionate than the one which he had delivered at Quilon.

> I suggest to you that the truth embedded in this very short *mantra* is calculated to satisfy the highest cravings of every human being—whether they have reference to this world or to the next. I have in my search of the scriptures of the world found nothing to add to this *mantra*... I feel that everything good in all the scriptures is derived from this *mantra*. If it is universal brotherhood... if it is unshakeable faith in the Lord and Master... if it is the idea of complete surrender to God ... then again I say I find it in this *mantra*... This *mantra* tells me that I cannot hold as mine anything that belongs to God, and if my life and that of all who believe in this *mantra* has to be a life of perfect dedication, it follows that it will have to be a life of continual service of our fellow creatures. This, I say, is my faith and should be the faith of all who call themselves Hindus.

How did Gandhi view Islam? Was he hostile to it? In what way did he differ from the orthodox Muslim view? Gandhi was often to face these questions. Thus, *Harijan* (July 13, 1940) carried an interesting—and revealing—peep into Gandhi's mind on the issue of Islam. A Muslim had written to him making the point that Muslims believed that the Prophet's life was wholly directed to God and truly non-violent, though not in the sense that Gandhi conveyed. As the questioner saw it, the Prophet never waged an offensive war and had the tenderest regard for the feelings of others, but when he was driven to a defensive war he drew his sword for a holy war and he permitted the use of the sword under conditions he had laid down. Said the questioner, "But your non-violence is different. You prescribe it under all conditions and circumstances. I do not think the Prophet would permit this. Whom are we to follow—you or the Prophet? If we follow you we cease to be Muslims. If we follow the Prophet, we cannot join the Congress with its creed of extreme non-violence. Will you solve this dilemma?" Gandhi gave a detailed answer. He told his questioner that since the latter saw the difference between what the Prophet said and what Gandhi said, the questioner "should unhesitatingly follow the Prophet" and not him. Nevertheless, said Gandhi, he could claim to have studied the life of the Prophet and the Koran as a detached student of religion.

Gandhi said that he must refuse to sit in judgement on what the Prophet did but must base his conduct on what the great teachers of the earth said, not on what they did. Gandhi further said that prophet-hood came not from the wielding of the sword, but from years of wrestling with God to know the truth. He added:

> Erase these precious years of the great life, and you will have robbed the Prophet of his prophethood. It is these years of his life which made Muhammad a prophet. A prophet's life, after he is acknowledged as one, cannot be our guide. Only prophets can weigh the work of prophets.

Gandhi was clear that just as a civilian could not judge the merits of a soldier, or a layman of a scientist, an ordinary man could not judge a prophet, much less imitate him. Gandhi reminded his questioner of what the Prophet said when he was asked why, if he could fast more than the prescribed number of times, his companions could not too. To which the Prophet's reply was, "God gives me spiritual food which satisfies even the bodily wants; for you He has ordained the Ramzan. You may not copy me."

Years earlier, on January 20, 1927, writing in *Young India* Gandhi had said that he regarded Islam to be a religion of peace. He had then said that he rejected the claim of *maulvis* to give a final interpretation to the message of Muhammad as he rejected that of the Christian clergy to give a final interpretation to the message of Jesus. Bluster, he said, was no religion nor was vast learning stored in capacious brains. The seat of religion, he concluded, was in the heart.

Gandhi had some problems with Sikhs. He did not see any difference between Sikhism and Hinduism and thought of them as "varieties of the same faith". He held that the Sikh gurus were all deeply religious teachers and reformers, and that they were all Hindus. But many Sikhs resented being called part of Hindus which, Gandhi said, he did not mind at all. Sikhs, he conceded, were free to regard themselves as distinct from Hindus. But he insisted that he held the *Granth Saheb* in "high reverence" because "so far as my reading of it goes it inculcates faith, valour and an invincible belief in the ultimate triumph of right and justice."

A Jain reader once admonished him for deliberately avoiding the subject of Mahavira in his writing. Gandhi had as much reverence for Mahavira as he had for the Buddha. Replied Gandhi, "I plead guilty to the charge of not being a Jain. But possibly I am a better informed devotee of Mahavira than many who claim to be Jains. If, however, I am not a devotee of Mahavira Swami, he or his devotees stand to lose nothing thereby. I alone will be the loser. I suggest that we merely betray our weakness when we resent the indifference of our neighbours about those whom we revere and idolize."

Gandhi was a firm believer in the importance and necessity of personal experience. In a dialogue with a Buddhist scholar Gandhi was to say, "For me there is nothing higher than what Buddha taught, and no greater master. For Buddha alone among the teachers of the world said, 'Don't believe implicitly what I say. Don't accept any dogma or any book as infallible.'"

The Buddhist scholar was emphatic in his belief that Buddha never prayed, but only meditated. Buddha only asked every person to find salvation for himself. Gandhi's reply was classic. He said, "Do not limit even the real Buddha by your own conception of Buddha. He could not have ruled the lives of millions of men that he did and does today if he was not humble enough to pray. There is something infinitely higher than intellect that rules us and even the sceptics . . . A merely intellectual conception of the things of life is not enough. It is the spiritual conception that eludes the intellect, and which alone can give one satisfaction." And much to the surprise of the scholar, Gandhi quoted Alexander Pope in regard to scepticism. Was it, asked Gandhi, of such people that Pope wrote:

> With too much knowledge for the sceptic side,
> With too much weakness for the stoic's pride,
> He hangs between; in doubt to act or rest;
> In doubt to deem himself a god or beast;
> To doubt his mind or body to prefer;
> Born but to die, and reasoning but to err;
> Sole judge of truth, in endless error hurled,
> The glory, jest and riddle of the world.

That Gandhi could so easily quote from English poetry often surprised many, but there were some verses, whether in English or in Hindi or in Sanskrit that he obviously could not but remember well. One of his favourite hymns was Cardinal Newman's famous *Lead, Kindly Light*.

> Lead, kindly light, amid the encircling gloom
> Lead thou me on;
> The night is dark, and I am far from home
> Lead thou me on.
> Keep thou my feet; I do not ask to see
> The distant scene; one step enough for me.

He knew many of Mirabai's *bhajans* and he was a great devotee of Tulsidas whose songs, too, he could recite by heart, like *Raghuvara Tumko Meri Laaj*, which he translated into English, and which, he said, he often hummed to himself at Satyagraha Ashram. As he once wrote: "The words of that hymn better express my state than anything else I can write." This is how his translation went:

> My honour, O God, is in Thy keeping;
> Thou art ever my Refuge,
> For Thou art Protector of the weak.
> It is Thy promise to listen to the wail of sinners;
> I am sinner of old, help me
> Thou to cross this ocean of darkness.
> It is Thine to remove the sin
> And the misery of mankind.
> Be gracious to Tulasidas
> And make him Thy devotee.

To the very end Gandhi lived in faith. It was indeed, the be-all and end-all of his very existence. Over and over again he would speak about a faith that moved mountains. A satyagrahi, he said, should have faith, because "without that faith, how can he undertake satyagraha?". In a speech he made in Masulipatam, he said, "Let your faith be not found wanting when it is weighed in the balance. That faith is of little value which can flourish only in fair weather. Faith in order to be of any value has to survive the severest trials. Your faith is a whited sepulchre if it cannot stand against the calumny of the whole world."

Faith, said Gandhi, "is the function of the heart" but it must be reinforced by reason for the two were not antagonistic as some believed. When faith became blind, it died.

5

A SPIRITUAL FORCE

What was Gandhi? A religious leader or a political revolutionary? Or was he both? In retrospect, he probably spoke more about religion and faith than about politics. In India, almost the first great speech he delivered was when he was tried on March 18, 1922, for "bringing or attempting to bring into hatred or contempt or exciting or attempting to excite disaffection towards His Majesty's Government established by law in British India and thereby committing offence punishable under Section 124A or the Indian Penal Code". Gandhi was tried in a court in Ahmedabad. After the charges were read out, Gandhi was asked whether he would plead guilty or ask to be tried. Gandhi unhesitatingly said, "I plead guilty to all the charges." A most remarkable thing to say. He went even further to say that the charges levelled against him by the advocate general were "entirely fair". He was rebellious but he said, "I wanted to avoid violence. Non-violence is the first article of my faith, it is also the last article of my creed." Terrific words that electrified his listeners. He had advocated non-cooperation with the government. By doing that he said he had "rendered a service to India and England by showing in non-cooperation the way out of the unnatural state in which both are living"—again most amazing words that few would have dared to utter. The British Government in India was evil, and non-violence implied voluntary submission to the penalty for non-cooperation with evil. A lesser person might have pleaded not guilty. But not Gandhi. He said, "I am here, therefore, to invite and submit cheerfully to the highest penalty that can be inflicted on me for what in law is a deliberate crime and what appears to me to be the highest duty of a citizen." But a greater challenge to the British government was still to come. Continued Gandhi, "The only course open to you, the Judge and the assessors, is either to resign your posts and thus dissociate yourselves from evil, if you feel that the law you are called upon to administer is an evil and that in reality, I am innocent, or to inflict on me the severest penalty if you believe that the system and the law you are assisting to administer are good for the people of this country, and that my activity is, therefore, injurious to the common weal." Powerful words that came from the depth of Gandhi's heart. The judge, Mr. C. N. Broomfield, had no option. He sentenced Gandhi to six years' simple imprisonment—the same sentence that Bal Gangadhar Tilak had received twelve years earlier for a similar offence. But Broomfield knew who Gandhi was. In awarding the sentence he said that he did not ignore the fact that in the eyes of millions of his countrymen Gandhi was a great patriot and a great leader, and that even those who differed from him in politics looked upon him as a man of high ideals and of noble and even saintly life. Judge Broomfield concluded in one famous line: "If the course of events in India should make it possible for the Government to reduce the period and release you, no one will be better pleased than I." No greater tribute could have been paid to Gandhi's non-violence.

And what did Gandhi do in jail? He spent six hours a day reading—mostly books on religion—and four hours spinning and carding, and told anybody who cared to listen to him that he was "as happy as a bird". Two years later, Gandhi was to be released but he bore no ill-will towards the British. Actually, the British did not quite know how to handle this man who seemed to be as much a saint as a politician. Lord Reading, who was then the viceroy of India, reported to London as follows: "I have always believed in his sincerity and devotion to high ideals but I have always doubted the wisdom of his political leadership." He campaigned for the removal of untouchability, but did not go very far. He advised Hindus that as the majority community they should show a spirit of generosity and give the Muslims a feeling of confidence and security by granting them the concessions that they wanted. That did not take the country very far either. But the British still held him in high regard. For example, Lord Irwin, who succeeded Lord Reading as viceroy, wrote: "I came to have no doubt whatever that if Mr. Gandhi gave me his word on any point, that word was absolutely secure and that I could trust implicitly." But then what else could anyone expect of Gandhi who vociferously held truth to be God?

Gandhi's devotion toward the eradication of untouchability was heroic. During the second Round Table Conference held in London in 1932, he had been greatly perturbed by Dr. B. R. Ambedkar's demand for separate electorates for the untouchables whom Gandhi called the Harijans—children of God. Should the British have conceded that demand, the Harijans would have been more than ever separated from the main body of Hindus. He was therefore strongly opposed to a separate electorate for the Depressed Classes. At first the British authorities were willing to listen to Gandhi. But later they reneged and threatened, as it were, to provide separate electorates to the Depressed Classes in what came to be known as the Communal Award. On hearing the news, Gandhi announced that as from September 20, 1932, he would undertake "a perpetual fast unto death" unless the British changed their mind. In a statement dated September 15, he explained to the public that the fast was intended above all "to sting Hindu conscience into right religious action" and "was resolved upon in the name of God, for His work and as I believe in all humility, at His call". Gandhi was then in jail. The British authorities offered to release him the day he went on fast. Gandhi wanted none of that. He only sought the grace of God and the blessings of friends like Rabindranath Tagore to whom he wrote a personal letter. Tagore promptly replied, "It is worth sacrificing precious life for the sake of India's unity and social integrity." Tagore added, "Our sorrowing hearts will follow your sublime penance with reverence and love."

Gandhi's "threat" to fast unto death if the Communal Award was not amended had its effect. Even Dr. Ambedkar was willing to accept a modification of it and signed what came to be known as the Poona Pact. Gandhi gave up his fast on the understanding, among other things, that caste Hindus would work towards "an early removal of all social disabilities imposed by custom upon the so-called untouchable classes, including the bar in respect of admission to temples". What followed then has been graphically described by Penderel Moon:

> In a wave of crusading enthusiasm that followed the fast, Untouchables were not only touched but embraced; in many places temples and wells were thrown open to them; a society known as "Servants of the Untouchables" was formed; an Abolition of Untouchability Week was held; money poured in, and an agitation was started for Gandhi's release to

enable him to throw himself in person into the anti-untouchability campaign.

Such was his determination to fight the curse of untouchability that in November of the same year he set out on a long Harijan tour of the country during which he travelled 12,500 miles and collected a sum of eight lakh rupees—a tremendous amount for those times.

There was one final occasion when Gandhi's total devotion towards non-violence and willingness to sacrifice himself at any cost for the greater good of the country and its people became manifest. And that was in August 1946-47. The Muslim League had called for Direct Action Day on August 16, 1946. It was a vicious call. Communal rioting broke out in Calcutta (Kolkata) far exceeding in scale and intensity anything of the kind that had been known before. According to official estimates some four thousand people were killed and over fifteen thousand were injured. In East Bengal, Muslim gangs went about killing and looting and even forcibly converting Hindus, abducting Hindu women and raping them. It was unbelievable. This had its own reaction in Bihar where thousands of Muslims, in turn, were killed with "revolting savagery" as one writer noted. Gandhi decided that he would move through the disturbed areas, alone and unprotected. The chief minister of Bengal then was a Muslim Leaguer, H. S. Suhrawardy. Many had blamed him for the rioting and killings. The need for restoring peace had never been felt as deeply as in those days of terror. How were those mad passions to be exorcised in Bengal, and especially in Calcutta? Gandhi offered to stay in Calcutta in an abandoned house in a notorious Muslim locality if Suhrawardy was willing to join him. Suhrawardy agreed and both moved into the Balliaghata area to stay in a place called Hydari Mansion amid filthy surroundings. The effect was miraculous. At first, hostile Hindu demonstrators threw stones at the house and broke windows. Gandhi came out to personally confront them and succeeded beyond measure. Thereafter, Hydari Mansion became practically a place of pilgrimage. Thousands of citizens poured in to seek Gandhi's advice and guidance.

Independence was to dawn one year later, on August 15, 1947. As if by magic, the tensions between Hindus and Muslims ceased. As Penderel Moon was later to write, Independence Day celebrations led to "unprecedented communal fraternisation". There was dancing in the streets of Calcutta, in which Hindus and Muslims joined, shouting "ek hogaye" (we have become one). Throughout August 1947, Gandhi continued to stay in Calcutta, holding prayer meetings in the evenings which drew both Hindus and Muslims. Such was the fraternisation and the establishment of peace that the then viceroy, Lord Mountbatten, wrote that while in the Punjab there were fifty-five thousand soldiers working at maintaining peace, in Calcutta, Gandhi was serving as "a one man boundary force". Shri C. Rajagopalachari, who was later to become the first Indian governor general of India, was to write: "Gandhi had achieved many things but there has been nothing, not even independence, which is so truly wonderful as his victory over evil in Calcutta."

That victory over evil was won not through force of arms but the force of non-violence and Gandhi's deep faith in God and true religion. But what did he mean by "religion"? He defined it in many ways throughout his life, at first in *Young India* and later in *Harijan* and, of course, in his many public utterances:

- Religion is that which changes one's very nature, which binds one indissolubly to the Truth within and which ever purifies. It is the permanent element in human nature which counts no cost too great in order to find full expression and which leaves the soul utterly restless until it has found itself.

- The root of religion is "that which binds". The root meaning of its Sanskrit equivalent, dharma, is "that which holds". It sustains a person as nothing else does. It is rock-bottom fundamental morality. When morality incarnates itself in a living man it becomes religion, because it binds, it holds, it sustains him in the hour of trial.

- Religion binds man to God and man to man.

- True religion and true morality are inseparably bound up with each other. Religion is to morality what water is to the seed that is sown in the soil.

- Belief in one God is the corner stone of all religions; the essence of all religions is one; only their approaches are different.

- The soul of religion is one, but it is encased in a multitude of forms.

- All religions enjoined worship of the one God who was all-pervasive. He was present even in a droplet of water or in a tiny speck of dust.

- The different religions are beautiful flowers from the same garden or they are branches of the same majestic tree.

- No religion is superior or inferior to another.

A Spiritual Force

Religion sustained Gandhi to the bitter end. When, on January 30, 1948, at his regular evening prayer meeting, Nathuram Godse shot him at close quarters, and he fell, his last words were "He Rama"—so characteristic of the Mahatma. Throughout his long life of seventy-eight years he had always relied on Rama. On that last day at Birla House in Delhi, it was with Rama on his lips that he breathed his last. As Penderel Moon was to note: "The apostle of non-violence had fallen a victim to violence, but his wish to die in harness with God's name on his lips, had been fulfilled." In his work on Gandhi, Moon has rightly summed up Gandhi's spirituality:

> Beyond question, he was a deeply religious man and lived, or aspired to live, "as ever in his great taskmaster's eye." His spirituality and frequent references to God were no mere pose, but sprang from genuine religious convictions; and, as he himself said, his experiments in the spiritual field gave him the power that he possessed for working in the political field.

There is no doubt that what made Gandhi such a powerful and potent force was the spiritual foundation that underpinned all his actions. In his quest for truth, and the realisation that truth was God, lay the path to achieving political, moral, and spiritual greatness. Would Gandhi, the politician, have succeeded without Gandhi, the saint? The answer is a definite no.

6

GANDHI AND GANDHIGIRI

All his life Gandhi pursued one thing: spiritualism. He was ever in quest of God. Whatever he did, or advocated, was based on that one single factor. And he was convinced about it. For him, Truth was God.

Gandhi was a unique phenomenon, a man of many parts. He combined political shrewdness with religious and moral ideals—a rare feat indeed. He took politics to India's villages and created a potent political force based on ahimsa and spirituality. As the British historian Arnold Toynbee pertinently noted: "After Gandhi, humankind would expect its prophets to live in the slum of politics."

Gandhi could have chosen to seek moksha for himself and leave the struggle for independence to others. But Gandhi would have none of it. His goal was to change society and use his own spiritual development for the good of humanity. He was as much in politics as he was in pursuit of God and there was no way of saying how to separate the two Gandhis. As Prof. Bhikhu Parekh writes: "He [Gandhi] was a man of action desperately anxious to acquire the enormous power he needed to change his society. It was, therefore, not enough for him to possess the powers naturally resulting from self-realisation. He had to be *sure* he had them, he had to *transform* them into political power, and he had to deploy them consciously to secure the desired political and social objectives."

The search for God was, however, the mainspring of all his actions. Gandhi once wrote: "What I want to achieve, what I have been striving and pining to achieve these thirty years [this he was writing in 1925] is . . . to see God face to face, to attain moksha. I live and move and have my being in pursuit of this goal. All that I do by way of speaking and writing, and all my ventures in the political field, are directed to this same end."

Given the circumstances, one wonders whether, if there was no Gandhi in the first quarter of the 20th century, there would have been need to invent one. What is true and has seldom been contradicted is that the times proclaim the man. In 1940, Britain needed Winston Churchill, not Neville Chamberlain. In 1920, India needed someone other than Bal Gangadhar Tilak (who was by then dead anyway) and that was Gandhi. Given India's long and painful history, would anybody, apart from a Gandhi, have been able to successfully combat the British?

Many questions remain unanswered. Could Gandhi have internalised his quest after the Supreme and led the Congress in secular terms? Then he would not have been a Gandhi. Could he have stuck to his quest but remained outside politics like a latter day Sant Tukarama or Kabir? Then India would have been bereft of a leader. Has Gandhi been really instrumental in changing Indian society? Perhaps Indian society would have changed even without a Gandhi because of the onset of technology and globalisation. All these issues may be highly debatable but what cannot be denied is the impact that Gandhi has had on people all over the world and the legacy he has left behind. It is a validation of Gandhi's philosophy that across the world social activists and leaders have chosen to follow his principle of militant non-violence. Martin Luther King Jr. was greatly influenced by Gandhi's ideology of non-violent social protest. The Dalai Lama has acknowledged the inspiration he has received from Gandhi's teachings. Nelson Mandela and Aung San Suu Kyi have fought oppressive regimes drawing upon Gandhi's legacy.

Gandhi had no intention of founding a new cult or establishing a following to preach his doctrine. In fact, he professed to a "horror of *'isms'*." He believed in the unifying nature of ahimsa and its power to create unity in diversity. A new cult would go against the very definition of ahimsa by further dividing people. He, therefore, discouraged people from deifying him in any way. "There is no such thing as 'Gandhism', and I do not want to leave any sect after me. I do not claim to have originated any new principle or doctrine; I have simply tried in my own way to apply the eternal truths to our daily life and problems . . . The opinions I have formed and the conclusions I have arrived at are not final. I may change them tomorrow." Gandhi never encouraged blind faith, insisting that every doctrine had first to be tested with reason before it was accepted.

If "Gandhism" was anathema to him, how would Gandhi have reacted to "Gandhigiri", the phenomenon that has recently swept the country thanks to Bollywood's *Lage Raho Munnabhai*? It is astounding that almost sixty years after the Mahatma's death his ideology has been brought back to life by making it applicable to our changing times. The film brings Gandhi and his ideals to the masses in a contemporary, acceptable format. It presents him, not as the grim, dour, to-be-revered personage of our history books, but as a "cool", practical, sympathetic man of exemplary stature whose philosophy has much to offer today's young generation.

As Gandhi always emphasised, satyagraha is not of the weak. Force is essential to overcome any wrong, except that the nature of the force has to be non-violent. And to be able to exert such force, as Gandhi did, one has to first rid oneself of all vestiges of violence. Gandhigiri, too, is about such a force—a moral force. It implies persuading the opponent to stop his wrong-doing or oppression by changing his very attitude. It is a fundamental, positive make-over of a person, which can only be accomplished through peaceful, non-violent means. Instances of people using Gandhigiri to redress difficult situations in their day-to-day lives have been reported from all over the country.

Whether Gandhigiri has come to stay, and how much it will succeed, only time will tell. Whether militant non-violence can become a successful weapon in combating the ills of a world greatly changed since Gandhi's times, remains a question mark. But the Mahatma would surely be happy to know that Indians have woken up to his philosophy and are assimilating it into their lives in whatever measure they can. After all, it was the dedicated, non-violent pursuit of the goal that mattered to Gandhi. Truth shall always remain truth, and what the Gandhigiri phenomenon clearly points to is the adaptability and relevance of Gandhi's ideas for all times. Gandhi's thought is visionary; his approach rational; his ideals universal; and his philosophy of truth and non-violence, manna for our troubled world. To quote the irreverently delightful words of the film: *Bande mein tha dum* (the man had guts), *Vande Mataram*.

Gandhiji's favourite bhajan
Vaishnava jana to

वैष्णव जन तो तेने कहीअे, जे पीड पराअी जाणे रे;

परदुःखे अुपकार करे तोये, मन अभिमान न आणे रे.

सकल लोकमां सहुने वंदे. निंदा न करे केनी रे;

वाच काछ मन निश्चल राखे, धन धन जननी तेनी रे.

समदृष्टि ने तृष्णा त्यागी, परस्त्री जेने मात रे;

जिव्हा थकी असत्य न बोले, परधन नव झाले हाथ रे.

मोह माया व्यापे नहि जेने, दृढवैराग्य जेना मनमां रे;

रामनामशुं ताळी लागी, सकळ तीरथ तेना तनमां रे.

वणलोभी ने कपटरहित छे, काम क्रोध निवार्या रे;

भणे नरसैंयो तेनु दरसन करतां, कुळ अेकोतेर तार्या रे.

BIBLIOGRAPHY

Andrews, C. F. *Mahatma Gandhi's Ideas*. London: George Allen and Unwin Ltd., 1929.
Desai, Mahadev. *The Gospel of Selfless Action.* Ahmedabad: Navjeevan publishing house, 1946.
Easwaran, Eknath. *Gandhi the Man*. Bombay: Jaico Publishing House, 1997.
Erikson, Erik H. *Gandhi's Truth*. New York: W. W. Norton & Company, 1969.
Fischer, Louis. *Gandhi: His Life and Message for the World*. New York: Signet Key Books, 1954.
Fischer, Louis. *The Life of Mahatma Gandhi*. New York: Macmillan, 1962.
Gandhi, M. K. *All Men are Brothers*. Paris: UNESCO, 1959.
Gandhi, M. K. *Collected Works of Mahatma Gandhi*. 100 vols. New Delhi: Publications Division.

Gandhi, M. K. *Food for the Soul*. Ed. Anand T.Hingorani. Mumbai: Bharatiya Vidya Bhavan, 1998.

Gandhi, M. K. *God is Truth*. Ed. Anand T.Hingorani. Mumbai: Bharatiya Vidya Bhavan, 1998.

Gandhi, M. K. *In Search of the Supreme*. 3 vols. Ed. V. B. Kher. Ahmedabad: Navajivan Publishing House, reprint 2002.

Gandhi, M. K. *My Varnashrama Dharma*. Ed. Anand T.Hingorani. Mumbai: Bharatiya Vidya Bhavan, 1998.

Gandhi, M. K. *The Law of Continence*. Ed. Anand T.Hingorani. Mumbai: Bharatiya Vidya Bhavan, 1998.

Gandhi, M. K. *The Story of My Experiments with Truth*. Ahmedabad: Navajivan Publishing House, 1927.

Jesudasan, Ignatius. *A Gandhian Theology of Liberation*. Anand: Gujarat Sahitya Prakash, 1987.

Kumar, Girja. *Brahmacharya Gandhi & His Women Associates*. New Delhi: Vitasta Publishing Pvt. Ltd., 2006.

Moon, Penderel. *Gandhi and Modern India*. London: The English Universities Press Ltd., 1968.

Narayan, Shriman. *The selected works of Mahatma Gandhi*. vols. 1 & 6. Ahmedabad: Navjeevan publishing house, 1968.

Parekh, Bhikhu. *Colonialism, Tradition and Reform*. New Delhi: Sage Publications, 1989.

Shukla, Chandrashanker. *Gandhi's View of life*. Bombay: Bharatiya Vidya Bhavan, 1968.

Tendulkar, D. G. *Mahatma*. 8 vols. Bombay: V. K. Jhaveri & D. G. Tendulkar, 1952.

About Indus Source Books

Indus Source Books is a niche, independent book publisher in Mumbai passionately committed to publishing good and relevant literature. We believe that books are one of the most important mediums of communication and we seek to bring out publications that help to serve the community and the world we live in.

At Indus Source Books, we celebrate the diverse spiritual traditions, culture, and history of the world and present it to our readers in a contemporary format that retains its essential flavour: "Indian Spirit, Universal Wisdom".

Visit our website www.indussource.com for more details.

Indus Source Books
PO Box 6194
Malabar Hill PO
Mumbai 400006
India
www.indussource.com
info@indussource.com